The Essential Enneagram

The Essential Enneagram

The Definitive Personality Test and Self-Discovery Guide

David N. Daniels, M.D.
and Virginia A. Price, Ph.D.

 HarperSanFrancisco
A Division of HarperCollinsPublishers

HarperCollins books may be purchased for educational, business, or sales promotional use. For information please write: Special Markets Department, HarperCollins Publishers, Inc., 10 East 53rd Street, New York, NY 10022.

HarperCollins Web site: http://www.harpercollins.com

HarperCollins®, ☕ ®, and HarperSanFrancisco™ are trademarks of HarperCollins Publishers, Inc.

FIRST HARPERCOLLINS PAPERBACK EDITION PUBLISHED IN 2000

Library of Congress Cataloging-in-Publication Data

The essential enneagram : the definitive personality test and self-discovery guide / David N. Daniels and Virginia A. Price.—1st HarperCollins pbk. ed.
   p.   cm.
  ISBN 0-06-25167-60 (pbk.)
  1. Ennegram. I. Daniels, David N., 1934– II. Price, Virginia Ann.

BF698.35.E54 E88 2000
155.2′6—dc21   00-022110

05 RRD(H) 30 29 28 27 26 25 24 23

Designed by J. Eagle

Contents

Acknowledgments • ix
Foreword by Helen Palmer • xi

Section 1: How to Discover Your Type • 1
What is the Enneagram? • 1
What is *The Essential Enneagram?* • 2
The Process of Self-Discovery and Self-Development
   Using *The Essential Enneagram* • 3

How to Begin • 4
Essential Enneagram Test Instructions • 4

Essential Enneagram Test • 5
Linking Paragraphs to Types • 9
The Enneagram Figure • 10

How to Proceed • 11
Understanding the Type Determination Pages • 11
   Figure 1—Layout of Type Determination Pages • 12
Detailed Explanation of the Type Determination Pages • 13
Understanding the Type Description Pages • 15
   Figure 2—Layout of Type Description Pages • 16
Detailed Explanation of the Type Description Pages • 17

How to Discover Your Type • 19
Type One: The Perfectionist • 20
Type Two: The Giver • 24

Type Three: The Performer   •   28
Type Four: The Romantic   •   32
Type Five: The Observer   •   36
Type Six: The Loyal Skeptic   •   40
Type Seven: The Epicure   •   44
Type Eight: The Protector   •   48
Type Nine: The Mediator   •   52

Summary of Type Discriminators   •   56

How to Confirm and Verify Your Type   •   70

How to Build Self-Understanding   •   71

Section 2: What to Do When You Have Discovered Your Type   •   73

Introduction   •   73

Part 1: General Practices and Principles for All Types   •   73
Breathing and Centering   •   73
Five General Principles   •   74
Principle I: Three Laws of Behavior   •   75
Principle II: Three Centers of Intelligence   •   76
Principle III: Three Life Forces   •   77
Principle IV: Three Survival Behaviors:
    The Personality Subtypes   •   79
Principle V: Three Levels of Knowing and Learning   •   80
Elements of Personal and Professional Development:
    the Nine Cs   •   82

Part 2: Specific Practices for Each Type   •   83
Practices for the Perfectionist (Type One)   •   84
Practices for the Giver (Type Two)   •   86
Practices for the Performer (Type Three)   •   88
Practices for the Romantic (Type Four)   •   90
Practices for the Observer (Type Five)   •   92
Practices for the Loyal Skeptic (Type Six)   •   94

Practices for the Epicure (Type Seven) • 96
Practices for the the Protector (Type Eight) • 98
Practices for the Mediator (Type Nine) • 100

Appendix A: Additional Enneagram Resources • 103
Appendix B: Validity of the Essential Enneagram Test • 107

Acknowledgments

We greatly appreciate all the individuals who participated in the development of *The Essential Enneagram*, originally published as the *Stanford Enneagram Discovery Inventory and Guide (SEDIG)*, especially the Enneagram teachers who participated in typing hundreds of individuals. Special thanks go to Judy Daniels for her many hours of technical support and encouragement.

Major assistance in writing, formatting, and editing was provided by Peter Enemark, Carolyn M. Dawn, and Kit Snyder. Assistance in technical and data analysis was provided by Ghassan Ghandour and Michael Menke.

Our original publisher, Robb Most of Mind Garden, Inc., provided inspiration and support as well as guidance in design and marketing. We extend our thanks to our publisher, Harper San Francisco, to John Loudon, Executive Editor, who helped us move forward with our work, to Terri Leonard, Managing Editor, who encouraged us along the way, and to Kris Ashley, Editorial Assistant, for her upbeat attitude and constant availability.

We used the methods of the oral tradition of Self-Discovery and the substantive way of understanding the Enneagram developed by Helen Palmer. *The Essential Enneagram* is based upon the understandings and philosophy of Helen Palmer, whose support, encouragement, and guidance we deeply appreciate.

David N. Daniels, M.D.
Virginia A. Price, Ph.D.

Foreword

The Essential Enneagram offers a groundbreaking and original approach to a key problem in personality study. How do you correctly find your place within a rich and complex system, when the choice itself requires knowing yourself beforehand? In bringing their combined talents and deep scholastic commitment to the question of self-identification, David Daniels and Virginia Price have made it a whole lot easier to correctly discover your Enneagram personality profile, thus opening a wealth of information for both psychological and spiritual development.

Their innovative method looks like a guided tour to discovering, confirming, and verifying your personality type. You are provided with key checkpoints along the way to make sure you stay on track, and a set of sensitive, practical exercises to aid your personal development once you've discovered your type. David and Virginia bring both scientific validity and reliability studies to the Enneagram. Their method of determining personality type is based on seven years of research with over 900 subjects.

In Section 1 they provide you with the user-friendly, short-paragraph test that their subjects used. They next show you the probability that the type you chose is correct, and probabilities are the absolute best that any depth psychometric instrument can provide. You are then shown how to confirm your choice, and exactly what steps to take if this checkpoint leads you to believe you are not the type you originally chose.

Once you're certain of your Enneagram profile, you move ahead to Section 2 where the authors give excellent daily practices that assist you in becoming more consciously aware of how your type is organized, its positive features, and how to break free of the limits your type imposes upon you. *The Essential Enneagram* is based on principles of self-awareness that I have long advocated. By providing elegant and precise descriptions of how different types of people are organized and motivated, this book guides you in exploring how your placement of attention and use of energy focuses your worldview, how you deal with stress and anger, and what you can do to develop yourself and receive support from others.

I first had the pleasure of teaching with David when we initiated the Enneagram Professional Training in 1988, using the panel method of personal inquiry. During our now many years of collaboration, I have consistently experienced his inspired clinical acumen, warmth and care, and profound understanding of human behavior and development. He is perhaps the most personally respected contributor in today's emerging field of Enneagram studies.

Virginia likewise brings extraordinary insight and clinical expertise to this work. For over 20 years she has pioneered and authored several works about the theoretical and practical aspects of modifying Type A personality behavior. Her research and clinical experience, her understanding of the theoretical basis of personality function, and excellent writing skills have contributed greatly to this field of study.

The section of this book entitled "What to Do When You Have Discovered Your Type" is rooted in David's and Virginia's extensive clinical experience and their understanding of people from the inside out. Their presentation of general methods for personal change and their type-specific practices are exceptionally valuable.

This long-awaited work is a must for anyone interested in effective communication, compassionate relationships, freedom from the confinement of repetitive behavior, and, ultimately, the freedom to be a complete human being.

Helen Palmer
January 2000
Berkeley, California

The Essential Enneagram

Section 1:
How to Discover Your Type

What Is the Enneagram?

The Enneagram is a powerful and dynamic personality system that describes nine distinct and fundamentally different patterns of thinking, feeling, and acting. Each of the nine patterns is based on an explicit perceptual filter. This filter determines what you pay attention to and how you direct your energy. Underneath each of the nine patterns is a basic proposition, or belief, about what you need in life for survival and satisfaction.

Each one of us developed one of the nine patterns to protect a specific aspect of our self that felt threatened as our personality was developing. As you discover your Enneagram personality type, you will discover more about your original whole self. You will also understand more about the unconscious motivation from which you operate. Discovering your Enneagram personality type can help you learn how to bring positive change into your life. It can help change the way you relate to yourself and others as well as give you a greater understanding of the circumstances and issues facing you.

What Is *The Essential Enneagram?*

We developed *The Essential Enneagram* as a simple and accurate way for you to identify your Enneagram personality type and as a guide for you to use to further your personal and professional development.

The Essential Enneagram Test consists of nine short paragraphs that describe the fundamentals of each of the nine personality types. You administer this test to yourself by reviewing the nine paragraphs and choosing the three paragraphs that seem most like you. Next you put the three selected paragraphs in order, beginning with the one that is the most like you. This process takes only a short time to complete.

You then proceed with an adventure in self-discovery by following the process described in *The Essential Enneagram.* This process guides you through the basic terminology of the Enneagram, the determination of your personality type, a comprehensive description of your type, the key discriminators differentiating each type from every other type, and a series of practices for self-development—including practices tailored specifically to your type.

A distinctive feature of the Essential Enneagram Test is the extensive research done to validate it. We conducted a validity study on just under 1,000 individuals. The results of the research show that the Essential Enneagram Test has a high level of validity and reliability. We have included a summary of this research in appendix B (pages 107 to 109).

By using *The Essential Enneagram* in the way described here, you can discover, confirm, and verify your Enneagram personality type with a high level of confidence. Please bear in mind that the purpose of the Enneagram and this book is not to label you but to aid you in your journey of self-understanding and self-development. By knowing your Enneagram personality type, you can become aware of the habits of your personality that limit you, and you can free yourself from those habits.

The Process of Self-Discovery and Self-Development Using *The Essential Enneagram*

The Essential Enneagram will guide you step-by-step through the process of taking the Enneagram personality test, discovering and confirming your correct type, and pursuing a path of self-development once you know your personality type. This page provides an overview of that process. When you have read this overview, turn the page and you will see how to begin.

Taking the Essential Enneagram Test

- First, you will read the Essential Enneagram Test instructions and take the test, which involves reading nine short paragraphs and choosing three of them.
- Then you will turn to page 9 to find out how the paragraphs you chose are linked to the Enneagram types.

Discovering and confirming your correct type

- The Type Determination pages and the Type Description pages are the two key tools you will use to discover and begin to confirm your type. You will find it useful to read the explanations of both the Type Determination pages and the Type Description pages.
- Then go to the Type Determination pages of the type associated with your first-choice paragraph. The Type Determination pages will guide you to the appropriate Type Description pages and provide instructions on how to proceed to confirm your correct type.
- You can further confirm your correct type by referring to the Summary of Type Discriminators, beginning on page 56.
- The final step in the process is to read How to Confirm and Verify Your Type on page 70.

What to do when you have discovered your type

- First, read the five general principles that apply to all nine Enneagram types and, follow, as desired, the practices based on those five principles.
- Then read and follow the four self-development practices associated with your specific type.

How to Begin

Read the instructions below, and complete the Essential Enneagram Test on pages 5 to 7.

Essential Enneagram Test Instructions

Following are nine paragraphs that describe nine different personality types. None of these personality types is better or worse than any other. Each paragraph is meant to be a simple snapshot of one of the nine Enneagram types. No paragraph is intended to be a comprehensive description of an individual's personality.

1. Read the descriptions and pick the three paragraphs that fit you best.
2. Number these paragraphs from 1 to 3 with 1 being the paragraph that seems most like you, 2 the paragraph next most like you, and 3 the third most like you.
3. Each of the nine paragraphs may describe you to some degree, but choose the three that seem most like you.

In making your selections, please consider each paragraph as a whole rather than considering each sentence out of the context of its paragraph. Ask yourself, "Does this paragraph as a whole fit me better than any of the other paragraphs?"

If you find it difficult to choose the three paragraphs most like you, think about which description someone close to you would select to describe you. Because personality patterns are usually most prominent in young adult life, you may also ask yourself which one of these patterns would best fit you in your twenties.

Recording your selections

After reading the paragraphs and selecting the three most like you, please record the paragraphs you selected:

1st choice: A B C D E F G H I
2nd choice: A B C D E F G H I
3nd choice: A B C D E F G H I

4. Once you have chosen the three paragraphs and recorded them, turn to page 9 to find out how those paragraphs are linked to the Enneagram types.

Essential Enneagram Test

A. I approach things in an all-or-nothing way, especially issues that matter to me. I place a lot of value on being strong, honest, and dependable. What you see is what you get. I don't trust others until they have proven themselves to be reliable. I like people to be direct with me, and I know when someone is being devious, lying, or trying to manipulate me. I have a hard time tolerating weakness in people, unless I understand the reason for their weakness or I see that they're trying to do something about it. I also have a hard time following orders or direction if I do not respect or agree with the person in authority. I am much better at taking charge myself. I find it difficult not to display my feelings when I am angry. I am always ready to stick up for friends or loved ones, especially if I think they are being treated unjustly. I may not win every battle with others, but they'll know I've been there.

B. I have high internal standards for correctness, and I expect myself to live up to those standards. It's easy for me to see what's wrong with things as they are and to see how they could be improved. I may come across to some people as overly critical or demanding perfection, but it's hard for me to ignore or accept things that are not done the right way. I pride myself on the fact that if I'm responsible for doing something, you can be sure I'll do it right. I sometimes have feelings of resentment when people don't try to do things properly or when people act irresponsibly or unfairly, although I usually try not to show it to them openly. For me, it is usually work before pleasure, and I suppress my desires as necessary to get the work done.

C. I seem to be able to see all points of view pretty easily. I may even appear indecisive at times because I can see advantages and disadvantages on all sides. The ability to see all sides makes me good at helping people resolve their differences. This same ability can sometimes lead me to be more aware of other people's positions, agendas, and personal priorities than of my own. It is not unusual for me to become distracted and then to get off task on the important things I'm trying to do. When that happens, my attention is often diverted to unimportant trivial tasks. I have a hard time knowing what is really important to me, and I avoid conflict by going along with what others want. People tend to consider me to be easygoing, pleasing, and agreeable. It takes a lot to get me to the point of showing my anger directly at someone. I like life to be comfortable, harmonious, and others to be accepting of me.

D. I am sensitive to other people's feelings. I can see what they need, even when I don't know them. Sometimes it's frustrating to be so aware of people's needs, especially their pain or unhappiness, because I'm not able to do as much for them as I'd like to. It's easy for me to give of myself. I sometimes wish I were better at saying no, because I end up putting more energy into caring for others than into taking care of myself. It hurts my feelings if people think I'm trying to manipulate or control them when all I'm trying to do is understand and help them. I like to be seen as a warmhearted and good person, but when I'm not taken into account or appreciated I can become very emotional or even demanding. Good relationships mean a great deal to me, and I'm willing to work hard to make them happen.

E. Being the best at what I do is a strong motivator for me, and I have received a lot of recognition over the years for my accomplishments. I get a lot done and am successful in almost everything I take on. I identify strongly with what I do, because to a large degree I think your value is based on what you accomplish and the recognition you get for it. I always have more to do than will fit into the time available, so I often set aside feelings and self-reflection in order to get things done. Because there's always something to do, I find it hard to just sit and do nothing. I get impatient with people who don't use my time well. Sometimes I would rather just take over a project someone is completing too slowly. I like to feel and appear "on top" of any situation. While I like to compete, I am also a good team player.

F. I would characterize myself as a quiet, analytical person who needs more time alone than most people do. I usually prefer to observe what is going on rather than be involved in the middle of it. I don't like people to place too many demands on me or to expect me to know and report what I am feeling. I'm able to get in touch with my feelings better when alone than with others, and I often enjoy experiences I've had more when reliving them than when actually going through them. I'm almost never bored when alone, because I have an active mental life. It is important for me to protect my time and energy and, hence, to live a simple, uncomplicated life and be as self-sufficient as possible.

G. I have a vivid imagination, especially when it comes to what might be threatening to safety and security. I can usually spot what could be dangerous or harmful and may experience as much fear as if it were really happening. I either always avoid danger or always challenge it head-on. My imagination also leads to my ingenuity and a good, if somewhat offbeat, sense of humor. I would like for life to be more certain, but in general I seem to doubt the people and things around me. I can usually see the shortcomings in the view someone is putting forward. I suppose that, as a consequence, some people may consider me to be very astute. I tend to be suspicious of authority and am not particularly comfortable being seen as the authority. Because I can see what is wrong with the generally held view of things, I tend to identify with underdog causes. Once I have committed myself to a person or cause, I am very loyal to it.

H. I am an optimistic person who enjoys coming up with new and interesting things to do. I have a very active mind that quickly moves back and forth between different ideas. I like to get a global picture of how all these ideas fit together, and I get excited when I can connect concepts that initially don't appear to be related. I like to work on things that interest me, and I have a lot of energy to devote to them. I have a hard time sticking with unrewarding and repetitive tasks. I like to be in on the beginning of a project, during the planning phase, when there may be many interesting options to consider. When I have exhausted my interest in something, it is difficult for me to stay with it, because I want to move on to the next thing that has captured my interest. If something gets me down, I prefer to shift my attention to more pleasant ideas. I believe people are entitled to an enjoyable life.

I. I am a sensitive person with intense feelings. I often feel misunderstood and lonely, because I feel different from everyone else. My behavior can appear like drama to others, and I have been criticized for being overly sensitive and overamplifying my feelings. What is really going on inside is my longing for both emotional connection and a deeply felt experience of relationship. I have difficulty fully appreciating present relationships because of my tendency to want what I can't have and to disdain what I do have. The search for emotional connection has been with me all my life, and the absence of emotional connection has led to melancholy and depression. I sometimes wonder why other people seem to have more than I do—better relationships and happier lives. I have a refined sense of aesthetics, and I experience a rich world of emotions and meaning.

IMPORTANT:

Please be sure you have completed
the Essential Enneagram Test
before reading any further.

Linking Paragraphs to Types

Find the types that correspond to each of the paragraphs you chose.

Test Paragraph	Enneagram Type	Type Determination Pages
A	Type 8	Pages 48–49
B	Type 1	Pages 20–21
(C)	Type 9	Pages 52–53
(D)	Type 2	Pages 24–25
E	Type 3	Pages 28–29
F	Type 5	Pages 36–37
G	Type 6	Pages 40–41
H	Type 7	Pages 44–45
(I)	Type 4	Pages 32–33

The Enneagram Figure

Ennea is Greek for nine, and *gram* means figure. The word Enneagram, then refers to a nine-pointed figure. It is usually shown inside a circle.

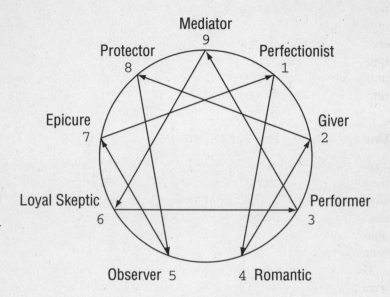

The arrows on this diagram indicate the stress and security types associated with each Enneagram personality type. The stress type is in the direction of the arrow and the security type is away from the arrow. See page 14 for an explanation of stress and security types.

How to Proceed

By this time, you have taken the Essential Enneagram Test and linked your first-, second-, and third-choice paragraphs to their respective Enneagram types.

Now you are ready to read the explanation of the Type Determination and Type Description pages, pages that are critical to determining your type. The Type Determination and Type Description pages are the main part of *The Essential Enneagram* guide to personality type. To identify, confirm, and verify your correct type, it is crucial to understand the terminology and the format of the Type Determination and Type Description pages.

Understanding the Type Determination Pages

The Type Determination pages tell you what the probability is that the paragraph you selected as your first choice is your correct personality type. It also tells you what the principal alternative possibilities are for your correct type given your first-choice paragraph. This quantitative information will help you determine your correct personality type.

The probabilities that appear on the Type Determination pages were discovered through extensive research conducted on the Essential Enneagram Test. A summary of that research can be found in appendix B (pages 107 to 109).

Figure 1 shows you the layout of the Type Determination pages. A detailed explanation of these pages follows figure 1.

Figure 1—Layout of Type Determination Pages

❶ **Type One: The Perfectionist**

❷ Type Determination

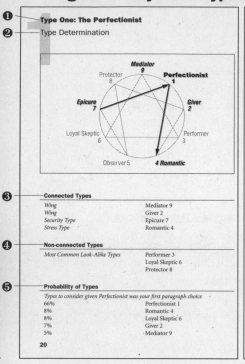

If you chose the Perfectionist paragraph as your first choice, there is a 66 percent probability that this is your type. Read the Perfectionist Type Description pages that follow to see if they accurately describe your personality. These pages can also help you gain insight into how you perceive the world and what you can do to enhance your personal development.

If you are not certain that the description of the Perfectionist type fits you, then consider your second and third paragraph choices and the other probable types identified on the facing page. Compare these types to the Perfectionist by reviewing the Type Description pages for your other likely possibilities.

To confirm your choice of type, or if you are still unsure, turn to the Type Discriminator pages beginning on page 56. These pages identify the characteristics that distinguish each type from every other type.

❸ **Connected Types**

Wing	Mediator 9
Wing	Giver 2
Security Type	Epicure 7
Stress Type	Romantic 4

❹ **Non-connected Types**

Most Common Look-Alike Types	Performer 3
	Loyal Skeptic 6
	Protector 8

❺ **Probability of Types**

Types to consider given Perfectionist was your first paragraph choice

66%	Perfectionist 1
8%	Romantic 4
8%	Loyal Skeptic 6
7%	Giver 2
5%	Mediator 9

20

21

❶ **Enneagram Type** Each Enneagram type is referenced by a number and a descriptive title.

❷ **Type Determination** These two facing pages help you determine which types are likely to be your actual type.

❸ **Connected Types** The four personality types that are associated with your basic type.

❹ **Non-Connected Types** The personality types that most often manifest characteristics similar to your basic type.

❺ **Probability of Types to Consider** The probability that you might be a type other than the one associated with your first choice paragraph.

A more detailed explanation is on pages 13 to 15.

Detailed Explanation of the Type Determination Pages

The following paragraphs refer to figure 1.

❶ Title of Type

❷ Type Determination

The first two facing pages for each type are labeled Type Determination because they help you determine if the type you chose as your first choice is your correct type. These pages show the probability of your being your first-choice type. They also show the probabilities that you might be another type, more specifically, the probability that you might be one of the *connected types* or one of the non-connected *look-alike types* associated with your first choice. You might also be your second- or third-choice type.

❸ Connected Types

Each Enneagram personality type has four connected types (the two wings, and the security and stress types). These are the four personality types associated with your basic personality type according to Enneagram personality theory. The Type Determination pages show what these four connected types are for each corresponding Enneagram type. Remember that you may be one of the connected types associated with your first choice.

Wings

Two of the connected types are called wings. They are the personality types on either side of your type on the Enneagram diagram. For example, if you are a Performer (Type Three), then the two personality types that are your wings are the Giver (Type Two) and the Romantic (Type Four). If you are the Mediator (Type Nine), then the two personality types that are your wings are the Protector (Type

Eight) and the Perfectionist (Type One). According to Enneagram theory, your personality type is influenced by one or both of the personality types that are your wings.

Security Type and Stress Type

The other two connected types are called the security type and the stress type. Your stress type is the personality type you shift into when you feel stressed and pressured or when you are mobilizing for action. *On the Enneagram figure, the stress type is indicated by the direction to which the arrow points.* Your security type is the personality type you shift toward when you feel relaxed and secure or, paradoxically, when you feel overwhelmed or exhausted. *On the Enneagram figure, the security type is the direction away from the arrow.* Each Enneagram type has its own security type and its own stress type. When you shift into your stress type or your security type, you may show either the higher qualities or the lower qualities of that type depending on the circumstances.

Although the existence of connected types influencing your actual personality type tends to complicate the process of identifying your correct type, their existence also makes the Enneagram system of personality a rich and dynamic system and helps account for the fact that each of us is uniquely different.

❹ Non-connected Types

Non-connected types are personality types on the Enneagram that can bear a definite similarity or look-alike quality to each other for some reason other than that they are wings or stress or security types. When you choose paragraphs on the Essential Enneagram Test that seem most like you, you may have inadvertently chosen one of your non-connected look-alike types instead of your actual type. The procedure described on the Type Determination pages will help you discover if a type you chose on the test is your correct personality type or a look-alike of your correct personality type.

❺ Probability of Types to Consider

Research with the Essential Enneagram Test shows the probability that you are a particular type given what paragraph you choose as your first choice. Each Type Determination section includes a table listing these probabilities For example, look at page 20, Type One. If 100 people chose paragraph B as their first choice on the Essential Enneagram Test, then 66 of those people would have Type One as their eventual correct type. However, 8 of the 100 people would eventually find that Type Four was their correct type, and another 8 would find that Type Six was their correct type. Furthermore, some others would discover that they are one of their lower probable types, their second or third choice, or a look-alike type.

Understanding the Type Description Pages

The Type Description pages provide you with a detailed description of the properties and characteristics of each of the nine Enneagram types. This qualitative information will help you confirm that you have selected your correct personality type. The wealth of information on the Type Description pages will help you understand your type more clearly and thoroughly. These pages also describe the path of personal development for each type.

Figure 2 shows you the layout of the Type Description pages. A detailed explanation of these pages follows figure 2.

Figure 2—Layout of Type Description Pages

① Type One: The Perfectionist

② Type Description

The Basic Proposition

The fundamental principle I lost sight of: ③	We are all one and are perfect as we are.
What I came to believe instead:	People are not accepted for who they are. Their good behavior is expected and taken for granted. Their bad behavior and impulses are judged negatively and punished.
The strategy I developed to cope with this belief:	I learned to gain love and self-regard by being good, responsible, and conscientious, doing things the correct way, meeting my high internal standards, and following the rules. I suppressed anger and developed tension and resentment.

Principal Characteristics ④

Because of this strategy, my attention is on:	Right and wrong, especially whatever is wrong that should be corrected. The rightness and wrongness of other people's behavior compared to mine. Self-criticism and others' criticism of me.
I put my energy into:	Getting things right. Issues about integrity. Maintaining standards judged to be important. Being responsible and self-reliant. Suppressing personal needs and natural desires.
I do everything I can to avoid:	Making mistakes. Being aggressive. Losing self-control. Violating social norms.
My strengths:	Integrity. Concern for improvement. Putting forth a lot of effort. Idealism. Self-reliance. Industriousness. Keeper of high standards. Self-restraint. Being highly responsible.

Stress and Anger ⑤

What causes me stress:	Not being able to quiet my internal critic and the associated anxiety and worry. Feeling overburdened by a sense of personal responsibility and conscientiousness. Too much error to correct. Too much that must be done right. Trying to let go of resentments and associated tension. Others blaming me or not taking responsibility for their mistakes.
What makes me angry:	Unfairness. Irresponsibility. Things being done the wrong way. The flagrant ignoring or disobeying of rules. Being unjustly criticized.
The nature of my anger:	Resentment. Self-justification. Tension and tightness. Outbursts of indignation.

Personal Development ⑥

The ultimate goal of my development:	To realize that we are all perfect as we are (complete and whole), that our worth and well-being are inherent and not dependent on our being right or wrong.
How I can further my personal development:	Appreciate that there is more than one right way and that others' "wrong" ways may simply be individual differences. Accept "imperfections" in myself and others. Practice forgiving myself and others. Allow free time for pleasure and relaxation. Question rigid rules and internal strictness. Use resentment as a clue to suppressed wants or needs. Integrate desires and natural impulses into my life.
What hinders my personal development:	My internal critic not accepting improvement as good enough or fast enough. Worry about getting it right leading to procrastination or too much attention to detail. Too much work and too little play.
How others can support my development:	Encourage me to go easy on myself and to take time for myself. Provide me with a nonjudgmental viewpoint. Remind me that the goal in life is to be human, not to be without fault.

① Enneagram Type Each Enneagram type is referenced by a number and a descriptive title.

② Type Description These two facing pages provide details of the personality type.

③ Basic Proposition Describes the evolution of how the personality type was formed.

④ Principal Characteristics Describes the basic characteristics associated with the strategy that the type developed.

⑤ Stress and Anger Describes the cause and nature of stress and anger for the type.

⑥ Personality Development Presents information about personal development for the type.

A more detailed explanation is on pages 17 and 18.

Detailed Explanation of the Type Description Pages

The following paragraphs refer to figure 2.

❶ Title of Type

❷ Type Description

The second two facing pages for each type are labeled Type Description pages because they describe each personality type in detail. These pages also include ideas about how to use knowledge of your personality type for self-development. Each of the Type Description pages follows a logical sequence, beginning with the basic proposition of each type.

❸ The Basic Proposition

The basic proposition consists of three parts:

The fundamental principle I lost sight of:	A basic truth about life that my early experiences and natural tendencies led me to lose sight of while my personality was forming.
What I came to believe instead:	The core belief that grew out of my early experiences and natural tendencies and that replaced the original fundamental principle.
The strategy I developed to cope with this belief:	The coping or survival strategy I developed because of this core belief in order to preserve a sense of safety, love, and value.

❹ Principal Characteristics

The second section of the Type Description pages describes the principal characteristics associated with the strategy each type developed.

Because of this strategy, my attention is on:	Whatever is required to support and sustain the particular survival strategy of my type.
I put my energy into:	Whatever is required by my habit of attention, since energy follows attention.

I do everything I can to avoid:	Whatever would threaten the basic survival strategy of my type.
My strengths:	The positive qualities that develop out of and are associated with the specific survival strategy of my type.

❺ Stress and Anger

The third section discusses the stress and anger associated with each type:

What causes me stress:	The situations and circumstances that cause stress and distress for my personality type.
What makes me angry:	The specific factors, usually hurts and experienced violations, that evoke anger in my type.
The nature of my anger:	The form the anger response takes depending on my type.

❻ Personal Development

The fourth section presents information about personal development for each type.

The ultimate goal of my development:	Remembering and recovering the fundamental principle I lost sight of during the development of my personality.
How I can further my personal development:	The type-specific awareness, steps, practices, and acceptance required to further my personal development. (See also the section called What to Do When You Have Discovered Your Type, which begins on page 73.)
What hinders my personal development:	The specific factors and resistance that impede my personal development.
How others can support my development:	The encouragement and actions others can provide me that are appropriate for my type.

How to Discover Your Type

Now, turn to the Type Determination pages associated with the Enneagram type that corresponds to your first-choice paragraph. There you will find instructions on how to proceed in discovering your type.

Keep an open mind as you proceed with discovering your type. Try to stay away from premature judgments; that is, wait until after you have read all the Type Description pages of your likely types. While the Essential Enneagram Test is highly accurate, it cannot guarantee that you will correctly select your personality type. Remember that your intuition can be a useful tool to help you know what your correct type is.

Continue your learning by confirming your type for yourself, verifying your type with others, and observing your own thoughts, feelings, and physical sensations. These processes are described under the heading How to Confirm and Verify Your Type, on page 70, and How to Build Self-Understanding, on page 71. You can also learn more about your Enneagram type from the books, tapes, and other Enneagram resources listed in appendix A (pages 103 to 105).

Then begin the work of personal and professional development using the knowledge of your Enneagram type. The section of this book labeled What to Do When You Have Discovered Your Type suggests a number of practices that will help you become more aware of how your personality functions, take action to change your habitual behavior, preview and review your progress in self-development, and reflect on the ultimate goal of your development.

Type One: The Perfectionist
Type Determination

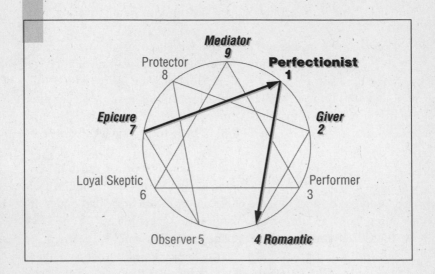

Connected Types

Wing	Mediator 9
Wing	Giver 2
Security Type	Epicure 7
Stress Type	Romantic 4

Non-connected Types

Most Common Look-Alike Types	Performer 3
	Loyal Skeptic 6
	Protector 8

Probability of Types

Types to consider given Perfectionist was your first paragraph choice

66%	Perfectionist 1
8%	Romantic 4
8%	Loyal Skeptic 6
7%	Giver 2
5%	Mediator 9

If you chose the Perfectionist paragraph as your first choice, there is a 66 percent probability that this is your type. Read the Perfectionist Type Description pages that follow to see if they accurately describe your personality. These pages can also help you gain insight into how you perceive the world and what you can do to enhance your personal development.

If you are not certain that the description of the Perfectionist type fits you, then consider your second and third paragraph choices and the other probable types identified on the facing page. Compare these types to the Perfectionist by reviewing the Type Description pages for your other likely possibilities.

To confirm your choice of type, or if you are still unsure, turn to the Type Discriminator pages beginning on page 56. These pages identify the characteristics that distinguish each type from every other type.

Type One: The Perfectionist

Type Description

	The Basic Proposition
The fundamental principle I lost sight of:	We are all one and are perfect as we are.
What I came to believe instead:	People are not accepted for who they are. Their good behavior is expected and taken for granted. Their bad behavior and impulses are judged negatively and punished.
The strategy I developed to cope with this belief:	I learned to gain love and self-regard by being good, responsible, and conscientious, doing things the correct way, meeting my high internal standards, and following the rules. I suppressed anger and developed tension and resentment.
	Principal Characteristics
Because of this strategy, my attention is on:	Right and wrong, especially whatever is wrong that should be corrected. The rightness and wrongness of other people's behavior compared to mine. Self-criticism and others' criticism of me.
I put my energy into:	Getting things right. Issues about integrity. Maintaining standards judged to be important. Being responsible and self-reliant. Suppressing personal needs and natural desires.
I do everything I can to avoid:	Making mistakes. Being aggressive. Losing self-control. Violating social norms.
My strengths:	Integrity. Concern for improvement. Putting forth a lot of effort. Idealism. Self-reliance. Industriousness. Keeper of high standards. Self-restraint. Being highly responsible.

Stress and Anger

What causes me stress: Not being able to quiet my internal critic and the associated anxiety and worry. Feeling overburdened by a sense of personal responsibility and conscientiousness. Too much error to correct. Too much that must be done right. Trying to let go of resentments and associated tension. Others blaming me or not taking responsibility for their mistakes.

What makes me angry: Unfairness. Irresponsibility. Things being done the wrong way. The flagrant ignoring or disobeying of rules. Being unjustly criticized.

The nature of my anger: Resentment. Self-justification. Tension and tightness. Outbursts of indignation.

Personal Development

The ultimate goal of my development: To realize that we are all perfect as we are (complete and whole), that our worth and well-being are inherent and not dependent on our being right or wrong.

How I can further my personal development: Appreciate that there is more than one right way and that others' "wrong" ways may simply be individual differences. Accept "imperfections" in myself and others. Practice forgiving myself and others. Allow free time for pleasure and relaxation. Question rigid rules and internal strictness. Use resentment as a clue to suppressed wants or needs. Integrate desires and natural impulses into my life.

What hinders my personal development: My internal critic not accepting improvement as good enough or fast enough. Worry about getting it right leading to procrastination or too much attention to detail. Too much work and too little play.

How others can support my development: Encourage me to go easy on myself and to take time for myself. Provide me with a nonjudgmental viewpoint. Remind me that the goal in life is to be human, not to be without fault.

Type Two: The Giver

Type Determination

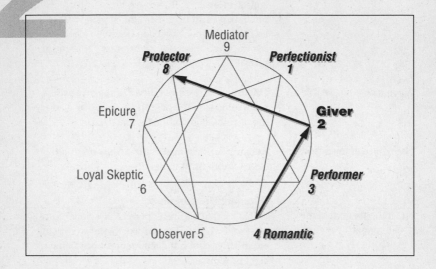

Connected Types

Wing	Perfectionist 1
Wing	Performer 3
Security Type	Romantic 4
Stress Type	Protector 8

Non-connected Types

Most Common Look-Alike Types	Epicure 7
	Mediator 9

Probability of Types

Types to Consider given the Giver was your first paragraph choice

65%	Giver 2
8%	Epicure 7
8%	Mediator 9
7%	Romantic 4
5%	Perfectionist 1

If you chose the Giver paragraph as your first choice, there is a 65 percent probability that this is your type. Read the Giver Type Description pages that follow to see if they accurately describe your personality. These pages can also help you gain insight into how you perceive the world and what you can do to enhance your personal development.

If you are not certain that the description of the Giver type fits you, then consider your second and third paragraph choices and the other probable types identified on the facing page. Compare these types to the Giver by reviewing the Type Description pages for your other likely possibilities.

To confirm your choice of type, or if you are still unsure, turn to the Type Discriminator pages beginning on page 56. These pages identify the characteristics that distinguish each type from every other type.

Type Two: The Giver

Type Description

	The Basic Proposition
The fundamental principle I lost sight of:	Everyone's needs are equally and freely met.
What I came to believe instead:	To get, you must give. To be loved, you must be needed.
The strategy I developed to cope with this belief:	I learned to get my personal needs fulfilled by being needed and by giving others what I feel they need and want, and I expect they will then do the same for me. I developed feelings of pride in being indispensable.

	Principal Characteristics
Because of this strategy, my attention is on:	The needs and wants of others, especially of people I care about and would like to have care about me. Relationships. The moment-to-moment feelings and emotions of others.
I put my energy into:	Sensing the emotional needs of others and doing what pleases them. Feeling good about being able to meet others' needs so well. Creating good feelings in others. Maintaining others' acceptance and approval. Romantic attachment.
I do everything I can to avoid:	Disappointing others. Feeling rejected or unappreciated. Dependence on others.
My strengths:	Being giving and helpful. Being generous. Sensitivity to the feelings of others. Being supportive. Being appreciative. Being romantic. High energy. Exuberance. Expressiveness.

Stress and Anger

What causes me stress: Feeling indispensable to too many people and projects. Confusion about my own needs. Trying to exercise my own freedom to be who I am and to take care of myself. Emotional upheavals resulting from investing so much in relationships, especially challenging ones.

What makes me angry: Feeling unappreciated or uncared for. Feeling controlled. Unmet personal needs and wants.

The nature of my anger: Intense, often sudden, emotional outbursts. Accusations. Crying.

Personal Development

The ultimate goal of my development: To realize that we are all loved for who we are, not for how much we give or how much we are needed by others; that the needs of all are invariably and ultimately met.

How I can further my personal development: Realize that being loved does not depend on changing myself for others. Maintain clarity about who the real me is. Notice and practice taking care of my own wants and needs. Use anger and rising distress as signals that I am not meeting my own needs. Acknowledge I am not indispensable and that is okay. Allow myself to receive from others. Practice setting limits and boundaries by saying no to requests from others, when appropriate. Notice when my helpfulness seems intrusive or controlling to others.

What hinders my personal development: Airtight rationalizations about what I have to do for others before I can do anything for myself. Pride that prevents me from admitting my own needs. Feelings of guilt about being selfish when I pay attention to my needs. Difficulty in receiving from others.

How others can support my development: Appreciate my independent self, instead of being seduced by or dependent on the help I give. Pay attention to my real needs and ask about them. Reinforce me for saying no when appropriate.

Type Three: The Performer

Type Determination

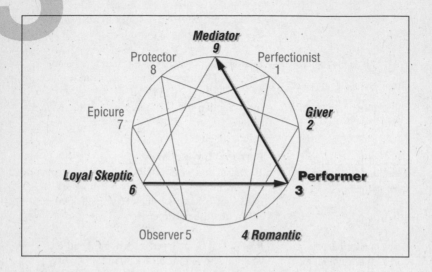

Connected Types

Wing	Giver 2
Wing	Romantic 4
Security Type	Loyal Skeptic 6
Stress Type	Mediator 9

Non-connected Types

Most Common Look-Alike Types	Epicure 7
	Perfectionist 1
	Protector 8

Probability Types

Types to consider given Performer was your first paragraph choice

54%	Performer 3
13%	Epicure 7
9%	Perfectionist 1
7%	Giver 2
5%	Protector 8
5%	Mediator 9

If you chose the Performer paragraph as your first choice, there is a 54 percent probability that this is your type. Read the Performer Type Description pages that follow to see if they accurately describe your personality. These pages can also help you gain insight into how you perceive the world and what you can do to enhance your personal development.

If you are not certain that the description of the Performer type fits you, then consider your second and third paragraph choices and the other probable types identified on the facing page. Compare these types to the Performer by reviewing the Type Description pages for your other likely possibilities.

To confirm your choice of type, or if you are still unsure, turn to the Type Discriminator pages beginning on page 56. These pages identify the characteristics that distinguish each type from every other type.

Type Three: The Performer

Type Description

The Basic Proposition

The fundamental principle I lost sight of:	Everything works and gets done naturally according to universal laws.
What I came to believe instead:	What gets done is dependent on each person's individual effort. People are rewarded for what they do, not for being who they are.
The strategy I developed to cope with this belief:	I learned to get love and approval by achieving success, by working hard to be the best, and by maintaining a good image. I developed a self-driving, go-ahead energy.

Principal Characteristics

Because of this strategy, my attention is on:	All the things that have to be done: tasks, goals, and future achievements. The most efficient solutions. How to be the best.
I put my energy into:	Getting things done quickly and efficiently. Staying active and busy. Competing. Achieving recognition and credit for accomplishments. Adjusting to whatever is required for success. Promoting myself. Looking good.
I do everything I can to avoid:	Failing to achieve my desired goals. Being overshadowed by others. Losing face. Uncomfortable feelings and doubts that arise from inactivity and slowing my pace. Whatever distracts me from getting things done, including emotions.
My strengths:	Being personable. Enthusiasm. Leadership. Self-assurance. Being practical, competent, and efficient. Inspiring hope. Poise.

Stress and Anger

What causes me stress:	The pressure that comes from basing how good I feel about myself on how much I get done and on status, prestige, and power. Not knowing my real feelings and values. Doing too much.
What makes me angry:	Obstacles: anything or anyone that threatens or thwarts the successful achievement of my goals. Incompetence. Indecisiveness. Inefficiency. Criticism.
The nature of my anger:	Impatience. Irritability. Occasional outbursts.

Personal Development

The ultimate goal of my development:	To realize that love comes from who we are, not from what we do, that everything that needs to be done gets done according to natural laws and does not depend on our individual effort.
How I can further my personal development:	Moderate my pace. Let my emotions surface. Ask myself what really matters. Practice looking inward for my own identity apart from success and the expectations of others. Set limits and boundaries on work. Allow myself to listen and be receptive. Realize that love comes from being, not from doing and having.
What hinders my personal development:	Impatience in dealing with my own and others' feelings. Working and overdoing to the point of fatigue and exhaustion. Not slowing down.
How others can support my development:	Encourage me to pay attention to feelings and relationships. Show me they care about me for who I am, not for what I have accomplished. Be supportive when I tell them what is really true for me. Let me know what is really important to them. Remind me to slow down and smell the roses.

Type Four: The Romantic

Type Determination

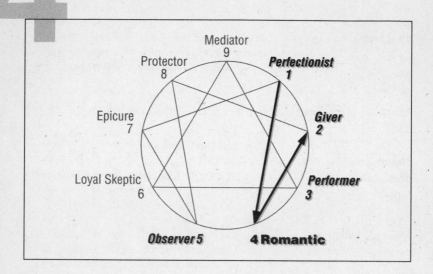

Connected Types

Wing	Performer 3
Wing	Observer 5
Security Type	Perfectionist 1
Stress Type	Giver 2

Non-connected Types

Most Common Look-Alike Types	Loyal Skeptic 6
	Mediator 9
	Epicure 7

Probability of Types

Types to consider given Romantic was your first paragraph choice

61%	Romantic 4
11%	Perfectionist 1
7%	Loyal Skeptic 6
7%	Mediator 9
5%	Epicure 7

If you chose the Romantic paragraph as your first choice, there is a 61 percent probability that this is your type. Read the Romantic Type Description pages that follow to see if they accurately describe your personality. These pages can also help you gain insight into how you perceive the world and what you can do to enhance your personal development.

If you are not certain that the description of the Romantic type fits you, then consider your second and third paragraph choices and the other probable types identified on the facing page. Compare these types to the Romantic by reviewing the Type Description pages for your other likely possibilities.

To confirm your choice of type, or if you are still unsure, turn to the Type Discriminator pages beginning on page 56. These pages identify the characteristics that distinguish each type from every other type.

Type Four: The Romantic
Type Description

4

	The Basic Proposition
The fundamental principle I lost sight of:	Everyone has a deep and complete connection to all others and all things.
What I came to believe instead:	People experience a painful loss of their original connections, leaving them feeling abandoned and feeling that they are missing something important.
The strategy I developed to cope with this belief:	I learned to keep searching for an ideal love or perfect circumstance to make me feel loved, whole, and complete again. I developed feelings of longing and envy for what was missing.

	Principal Characteristics
Because of this strategy, my attention is on:	What is positive and attractive about the future and the past. What is missing or distant that I long for and feel lonely without. What is aesthetically pleasing and deeply touching or meaningful.
I put my energy into:	Intense feelings of sadness and longing, associated with what seems to be missing or lacking in my life. Finding love, meaning, and fulfillment through self-expression and deep connection. Creating myself to be a unique individual.
I do everything I can to avoid:	Being rejected, abandoned, not heard, or insignificant. Feeling I do not measure up. Feeling there is something wrong with me. The mundane. People and experiences that lack emotional depth.
My strengths:	Sensitivity. A creative orientation. Being attuned to feelings. A capacity to empathize with suffering. Intensity. Passion. Romantic idealism. Emotional depth. Authenticity. Introspection.

Stress and Anger

What causes me stress: People and experiences not living up to my romantic ideals or desire for intensity. Wanting more than is available. Envying what others have that I do not have or what they are that I am not. Unmanageable feelings, especially in emotional crises.

What makes me angry: · People who disappoint me, let me down, or leave me. Remembering such people from my past. Being slighted, rejected, abandoned. Feeling misunderstood. Phoniness and insincerity.

The nature of my anger: Fiery outbursts or dissolving into tears. Depression.

Personal Development

The ultimate goal of my development: To realize that in the present moment we are loved and completely whole, lacking no essential quality or ingredient, that we are interconnected and at one with all life.

How I can further my personal development: Focus on what is positive in life right now rather than on what is missing. Maintain a consistent course of action despite fluctuating and intense feelings. Participate in physical activity and helping others in order to become less self-absorbed. Delay reacting until intense emotions begin to subside. Appreciate ordinary everyday experiences.

What hinders my personal development: Letting my strong feelings run the show and falling into inaction. Resisting changing "who I am" for fear of losing my individuality. Feeling I won't measure up. Feeling the world will let me down. Getting self-absorbed. Downplaying improvement that is not dramatic and becoming discouraged.

How others can support my development: Encourage me to keep my attention on what is positive in the present. Honor my feelings and my idealism. Reveal their real feelings and true reactions. Let me see that they really understand me instead of trying to change me.

Type Five: The Observer

Type Determination

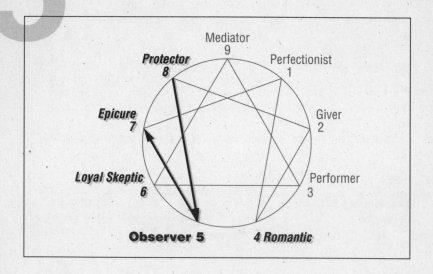

Connected Types

Wing	Romantic 4
Wing	Loyal Skeptic 6
Security Type	Protector 8
Stress Type	Epicure 7

Non-connected Types

Most Common Look-Alike Types	Perfectionist 1
	Mediator 9

Probability of Types

Types to consider given Observer was your first paragraph choice

65%	Observer 5
11%	Loyal Skeptic 6
11%	Mediator 9

If you chose the Observer paragraph as your first choice, there is a 65 percent probability that this is your type. Read the Observer Type Description pages that follow to see if they accurately describe your personality. These pages can also help you gain insight into how you perceive the world and what you can do to enhance your personal development.

If you are not certain that the description of the Observer type fits you, then consider your second and third paragraph choices and the other probable types identified on the facing page. Compare these types to the Observer by reviewing the Type Description pages for your other likely possibilities.

To confirm your choice of type, or if you are still unsure, turn to the Type Discriminator pages beginning on page 56. These pages identify the characteristics that distinguish each type from every other type.

Type Five: The Observer

Type Description

	The Basic Proposition
The fundamental principle I lost sight of:	There is an ample supply of all the knowledge and energy everyone needs.
What I came to believe instead:	The world demands too much from people and gives them too little.
The strategy I developed to cope with this belief:	I learned to protect myself from intrusive demands and being drained of my resources by becoming private and self-sufficient. I do this by limiting my desires and wants and by accumulating a lot of knowledge. I developed a sense of avarice, but only for things I could not do without.

	Principal Characteristics
Because of this strategy, my attention is on:	The intellectual domain. Facts. Analysis and compartmentalized thinking. Intrusions or demands on me.
I put my energy into:	Observing from a detached stance. Learning all there is to know about a subject. Thinking and analyzing in advance. Dampening and reducing feelings. Self-containment, withdrawing, conserving. Maintaining sufficient privacy, boundaries, and limits.
I do everything I can to avoid:	Strong feelings, especially fear. Intrusive or demanding people or circumstances. Feelings of inadequacy and emptiness.
My strengths:	Scholarliness. Being knowledgeable. Thoughtfulness. Calmness in crisis. Being respectful. Keeping confidences. Dependability. Appreciation of simplicity.

Stress and Anger

What causes me stress: Failing to maintain sufficient privacy, boundaries, and limits. Becoming fatigued. Having desires, needs, and wants that lead to dependency. Trying to learn everything there is to know before taking action.

What makes me angry: Being considered factually incorrect. Demands, intrusions. An overload of emotional input. Not having the opportunity for enough private time to restore my energy.

The nature of my anger: Self-containment and withholding. Tension and disapproval. Short bursts of temper.

Personal Development

The ultimate goal of my development: To realize that there is a natural and sufficient supply of what is needed to support and sustain life, that staying engaged in life will not deplete our resources and energy.

How I can further my personal development: Allow myself to experience feelings instead of detaching and retreating into my mind. Recognize that withdrawing and withholding invite intrusion. Take action, realizing that I have ample energy and support to carry it off. Participate in physical activity. Find ways to engage in conversation, to express myself, and to reveal personal matters.

What hinders my personal development: Minimizing needs and detaching from the ongoing flow of life. Missing opportunities to do things with others. Isolating myself from my feelings and from connecting with others. Not recognizing fear or anger in myself. Reluctance to discuss and reveal personal matters. Excessive analysis.

How others can support my development: Respect my need for privacy and space. Make clear distinctions between requests and demands. Provide moderate feedback about their own feelings and concerns. Encourage me to be self-disclosing and to express my feelings in the here and now. Appreciate my sensitivity. Appreciate my ability to live and let live.

Type Six: The Loyal Skeptic

Type Determination

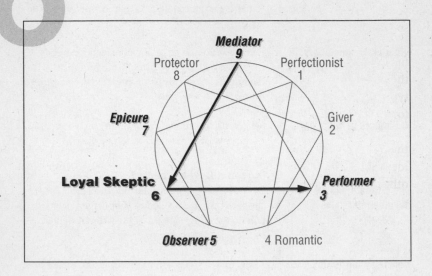

Connected Types

Wing	Observer 5
Wing	Epicure 7
Security Type	Mediator 9
Stress Type	Performer 3

Non-connected Types

Most Common Look-Alike Types	Romantic 4

Probability of Types

Types to consider given Loyal Skeptic was your first paragraph choice

66%	Loyal Skeptic 6
8%	Observer 5
8%	Mediator 9
5%	Romantic 4
5%	Epicure 7

If you chose the Loyal Skeptic paragraph as your first choice, there is a 66 percent probability that this is your type. Read the Loyal Skeptic Type Description pages that follow to see if they accurately describe your personality. These pages can also help you gain insight into how you perceive the world and what you can do to enhance your personal development.

If you are not certain that the description of the Loyal Skeptic type fits you, then consider your second and third paragraph choices and the other probable types identified on the facing page. Compare these types to the Loyal Skeptic by reviewing the Type Description pages for your other likely possibilities.

To confirm your choice of type, or if you are still unsure, turn to the Type Discriminator pages beginning on page 56. These pages identify the characteristics that distinguish each type from every other type.

Type Six: The Loyal Skeptic

Type Description

	The Basic Proposition
The fundamental principle I lost sight of:	We all begin with faith in ourselves, in others, and in the universe.
What I came to believe instead:	The world is threatening and dangerous, and people just can't trust one another.
The strategy I developed to cope with this belief:	*Phobic Stance:* While I became fearful and doubting and hence learned to be vigilant and questioning, I also learned to obey authority, to escape perceived threats and dangers, to gain security, and to avoid hazards. *Counterphobic stance:* While I became fearful and doubting and hence learned to be vigilant and questioning, I also learned to defy authority, to battle perceived threats and dangers, to defy security, and to face hazards.
	Principal Characteristics
Because of this strategy, my attention is on:	What could go wrong or be dangerous. Potential pitfalls, difficulties, incongruities. Implications, inferences, and hidden meanings.
I put my energy into:	Doubting, testing, and looking for double messages. Logical analysis to figure things out. Playing the devil's advocate. Ambivalence toward authority. Showing strength. Gaining security by obtaining the goodwill of others, being loyal to others, and dedicating myself to worthy causes.
I do everything I can to avoid:	Being helpless or not in control in the face of danger and harm. Succumbing to danger or harm. Getting stuck in doubt and contrary thinking. Alienating people I depend on by contradicting or opposing them.
My strengths:	Trustworthiness. Loyalty. Thoughtfulness. Questioning mind. Warmth. Perseverance. Responsibility. Protectiveness. Intuition. Wit. Sensitivity.

Stress and Anger

What causes me stress: The pressure I put on myself in my efforts to deal with uncertainty and insecurity. Difficulties with authority, either excessive obedience or rebellion. Trying to maintain the trust and goodwill of others while experiencing mistrust and ambivalence toward them.

What makes me angry: Untrustworthiness, betrayal. Feeling cornered, controlled, or pressured. Interactions with others that feel too demanding. Others' lack of responsiveness to me.

The nature of my anger: Wit. Sarcasm. Biting remarks. Accusations. Defensive lashing out.

Personal Development

The ultimate goal of my development: To realize that it is natural to have faith in ourselves and one another, that we can embrace and support life without doubt and mistrust.

How I can further my personal development: Be and act as my own authority. Reclaim faith in myself, others, and the universe. Accept that some uncertainty and insecurity are a natural part of life. Check out my fears and concerns with others. Recognize that staying busy is a way to reduce awareness of anxiety. Recognize that both fight and flight are reactions to fear. Move ahead with positive action in spite of the presence of fear.

What hinders my personal development: Doubt and ambivalence. Wanting too much certainty. Being overly controlling or overprotective. Disbelief in my own capacities and decisions. Letting worst-case scenarios dominate my thinking.

How others can support my development: Be consistent and trustworthy with me. Be self-disclosing and encourage me to be self-disclosing. Counter my doubts and fears with positive and reassuring alternatives that are realistic.

Type Determination

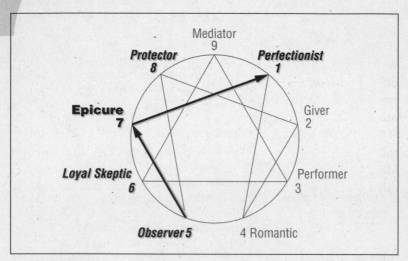

Connected Types

Wing	Loyal Skeptic 6
Wing	Protector 8
Security Type	Observer 5
Stress Type	Perfectionist 1

Non-connected Types

Most Common Look-Alike Types	Giver 2
	Performer 3
	Mediator 9

Probability of Types

Types to consider given Epicure was your first paragraph choice

52%	Epicure 7
8.5%	Protector 8
7%	Giver 2
7%	Observer 5
7%	Loyal Skeptic 6
6%	Mediator 9
5.5%	Perfectionist 1

If you chose the Epicure paragraph as your first choice, there is a 52 percent probability that this is your type. Read the Epicure Type Description pages that follow to see if they accurately describe your personality. These pages can also help you gain insight into how you perceive the world and what you can do to enhance your personal development.

If you are not certain that the description of the Epicure type fits you, then consider your second and third paragraph choices and the other probable types identified on the facing page. Compare these types to the Epicure by reviewing the Type Description pages for your other likely possibilities.

To confirm your choice of type, or if you are still unsure, turn to the Type Discriminator pages beginning on page 56. These pages identify the characteristics that distinguish each type from every other type.

Type Seven: The Epicure

Type Description

The Basic Proposition

The fundamental principle I lost sight of:	Life is a full spectrum of possibilities to be experienced freely and with sustained concentration.
What I came to believe instead:	The world limits people, frustrates them, and causes them pain.
The strategy I developed to cope with this belief:	I learned to protect myself from limitations and pain by engaging in pleasurable activities and by imagining many fascinating possibilities for the future. I became a glutton for interesting ideas and experiences.

Principal Characteristics

Because of this strategy, my attention is on:	Interesting, pleasurable, and fascinating ideas, plans, options, projects. Interconnections and interrelationships among diverse areas of information and knowledge. What I want.
I put my energy into:	Enjoying and experiencing life to its fullest. Keeping options open and life upbeat. An active imagination. Being liked (charming and disarming). Maintaining a privileged position.
I do everything I can to avoid:	Frustrations, constraints, and limitations. Painful situations or feelings. Boredom.
My strengths:	Playfulness. Inventiveness. Being enjoyable and upbeat. High energy. Optimism. Love of life. Vision. Enthusiasm. Helpfulness. Imagination.

Stress and Anger

What causes me stress: Coping with the overload that results from trying to sample all that life has to offer. Making the same mistakes over and over because of my desire to avoid pain. Making commitments and then feeling trapped by them.

What makes me angry: Constraints or limits that prevent me from getting what I want. People who are often stuck, unhappy, depressed, or blaming others.

The nature of my anger: Brief and to the point. Short-lived. Episodic. Impetuous.

Personal Development

The ultimate goal of my development: To realize that in order to experience life fully we must be consciously present in the here and now; that we support and sustain ourselves and others by cultivating this conscious presence.

How I can further my personal development: Notice when seeking pleasurable options is a response to fear of deprivation, a desire to escape from responsibilities that constrain my freedom, or an escape from pain. Practice working on one thing at a time until it is completed. Live life more fully in the present moment and less in the future. Appreciate more deeply the feelings and concerns of others. Realize that it is limiting to seek just the positive and avoid the negative.

What hinders my personal development: A preoccupation with myself and what I want. Difficulty acknowledging anything negative about myself. Unwillingness to take steps that involve experiencing pain or conflict. Being easily distracted and diverted from deeper purposes and commitments.

How others can support my development: Support me when I slow down and stick with commitments. Let me know what their needs and wants are and how important their needs and wants are to them. Encourage me to deal with pain, fear, and restlessness rather than escaping from these.

Type Eight: The Protector

Type Determination

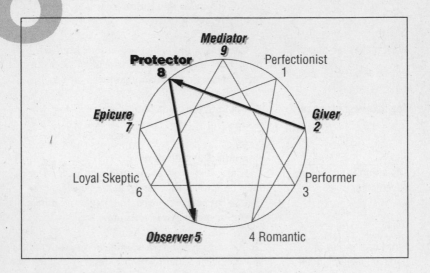

Connected Types

Wing	Epicure 7
Wing	Mediator 9
Security Type	Giver 2
Stress Type	Observer 5

Non-connected Types

Most Common Look-Alike Types	Perfectionist 1
	Romantic 4
	Loyal Skeptic 6

Probability of Types

Types to consider given Protector was your first paragraph choice

37%	Protector 8
16.5%	Loyal Skeptic 6
16%	Perfectionist 1
8%	Romantic 4
7%	Epicure 7
6%	Mediator 9

If you chose the Protector paragraph as your first choice, there is a 37 percent probability that this is your type. Read the Protector Type Description pages that follow to see if they accurately describe your personality. These pages can also help you gain insight into how you perceive the world and what you can do to enhance your personal development.

If you are not certain that the description of the Protector type fits you, then consider your second and third paragraph choices and the other probable types identified on the facing page. Compare these types to the Protector by reviewing the Type Description pages for your other likely possibilities.

To confirm your choice of type, or if you are still unsure, turn to the Type Discriminator pages beginning on page 56. These pages identify the characteristics that distinguish each type from every other type.

Type Eight: The Protector

Type Description

	The Basic Proposition
The fundamental principle I lost sight of:	Everyone begins in innocence and without guile, and everyone can sense truth.
What I came to believe instead:	It is a hard and unjust world in which the powerful take advantage of others' innocence.
The strategy I developed to cope with this belief:	I learned to become strong and powerful by imposing my own truth and by hiding my vulnerability in order to protect myself and others and to gain others' respect. I developed a forceful energy and came to rely on my own instincts.
	Principal Characteristics
Because of this strategy, my attention is on:	Power and control. Justice and injustice. Deceptions and manipulations. All-or-nothing polarities. Whatever demands action right now.
I put my energy into:	Control and dominance of my space and of the people and things in my space. Taking direct action and facing conflict. Protecting the weak and innocent. Gaining respect by being strong and just.
I do everything I can to avoid:	Being weak, vulnerable, uncertain, or dependent. Losing the regard of people I respect.
My strengths:	Courage. Persistence. Fairness. Decisiveness. Protectiveness. Self-assertion. Intensity. Friendliness. Magnanimity. The ability to energize others.

Stress and Anger

What causes me stress: Being unable to correct perceived injustice. Having to contain my confrontational style and having difficulty containing it. Going full-out and denying fatigue and pain.

What makes me angry: Deceit. Manipulation. People who won't stand up for themselves. Others not responding to me or to what has to be done. Boundaries or rules that are unjust or too constraining. Attempts to control me.

The nature of my anger: Powerful anger expressed in direct, confrontational style or armored withdrawal. Balancing the books (revenge).

Personal Development

The ultimate goal of my development: To realize that we are all inherently innocent and can naturally sense truth; that approaching each situation with a fresh perspective and free of personal prejudice enables us to recognize truth.

How I can further my personal development: Notice my intensity and its impact on others. Treat my intensity as an attempt to mask my vulnerability. Treat what seems like weakness as progress in letting myself experience vulnerability and tender feelings. Practice waiting and listening before taking action as a way to moderate my impulsivity. Apply only the appropriate amount of force in each situation. Welcome a sense of calm and quiet within. Seek win-win solutions. Learn to compromise.

What hinders my personal development: Refusing to be controlled and being unaware of controlling others. Excessive lifestyle that leads to exhaustion and alienation of others. Self-defeating behaviors. Denial of my fears, weaknesses, and vulnerability. Not valuing my own tenderness and sensitivity.

How others can support my development: Stand their ground. Stay firm. Be forthright. Speak their own truth. Provide feedback about my impact on them. Support me when I reveal softer feelings and vulnerabilities.

Type Nine: The Mediator
Type Determination

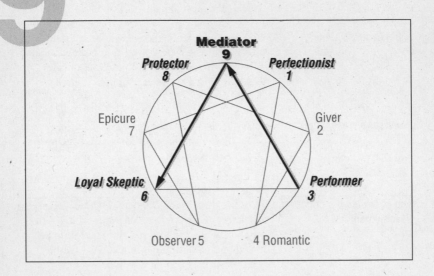

Connected Types

Wing	Protector 8
Wing	Perfectionist 1
Security Type	Performer 3
Stress Type	Loyal Skeptic 6

Non-connected Types

Most Common Look-Alike Types	Giver 2
	Romantic 4
	Epicure 7

Probability of Types

Types to consider given Mediator was your first paragraph choice

68%	Mediator 9
7%	Perfectionist 1
6%	Giver 2
5%	Loyal Skeptic 6
5%	Epicure 7

If you chose the Mediator paragraph as your first choice, there is a 68 percent probability that this is your type. Read the Mediator Type Description pages that follow to see if they accurately describe your personality. These pages can also help you gain insight into how you perceive the world and what you can do to enhance your personal development.

If you are not certain that the description of the Mediator type fits you, then consider your second and third paragraph choices and the other probable types identified on the facing page. Compare these types to the Mediator by reviewing the Type Description pages for your other likely possibilities.

To confirm your choice of type, or if you are still unsure, turn to the Type Discriminator pages beginning on page 56. These pages identify the characteristics that distinguish each type from every other type.

Type Nine: The Mediator

Type Description

9

	The Basic Proposition
The fundamental principle I lost sight of:	Everyone belongs equally in a state of unconditional love and union.
What I came to believe instead:	The world treats people as unimportant for what they are, and requires them to blend in as the way to experience a sense of comfort and belonging.
The strategy I developed to cope with this belief:	I learned to forget myself and merge with others. I substituted inessentials and small comforts for real priorities.

	Principal Characteristics
Because of this strategy, my attention is on:	Others' agendas, requests, and demands. All the things in the environment that beckon.
I put my energy into:	Being sensitive to others and trying to please them. Keeping life comfortable and familiar. Maintaining structure and routine so that life will be predictable. Maintaining peace and quiet. Containing anger. Doing the less essential and comforting activities rather than the more important and more disturbing ones.
I do everything I can to avoid:	Conflict, confrontation, feeling uncomfortable. Too many competing demands on my attention and energy.
My strengths:	Attentiveness to others. Empathy. Supportiveness. Accountability. Steadfastness. Being adaptive. Being accepting. Being receptive. Being caring.

Stress and Anger

What causes me stress:	Taking a position. Saying no to someone and having that person get angry. Having to make timely decisions and set priorities. Dealing with a commitment I made that I didn't really want to make.
What makes me angry:	Being treated as not important. Feeling controlled by others. Being forced to face conflict.
The nature of my anger:	Passive aggression, manifested as stubbornness or resistance. Occasionally "boiling over" and exploding.

Personal Development

The ultimate goal of my development:	To realize that we all are unconditionally and equally loved (accepted and appreciated for who we are as individuals), that our worth and well-being come from within.
How I can further my personal development:	Pay attention to my own needs and well-being. Use anger as a signal of feeling discounted and remind myself that I really do matter. Notice feelings I may be blocking out when I turn from my real priorities to substitutes, such as TV, food, errands, or chores. Notice when my prolonged ruminating keeps me from setting priorities and taking action on them. Accept discomfort and change as a natural part of life. Practice loving myself as well as I love others.
What hinders my personal development:	Feeling that I don't count. Feeling that I don't deserve to pursue my own agenda. Giving everything equal importance and, consequently, missing my real priorities. Avoiding the discomfort and disruption required for change.
How others can support my development:	Encourage me to express my own position. Ask me what I want and what is good for me, and give me time to figure out the answer. Support me when I act responsibly toward myself. Allow me to acknowledge my anger. Encourage me to set and keep my own boundaries, limits, and priorities.

Summary of Type Discriminators

Following are the shared characteristics and the key discriminators for each pair of the *connected* and *non-connected* types on the Enneagram, thirty-six in all. The connected types are those that share a wing with each other or that have a security-stress connection. Non-connected types often share certain characteristics that make them look alike, too.

W The two types are *wings*.

S The types are *security and stress* types of each other.

L The two types are non-connected types that look alike.

W Types One and Two. Perfectionists and Givers look alike because as wings of each other they possess some of the same personality traits. Both can have high standards of giving, focus intense energy on the improvement or well-being of others, and know what is best for others. Both types definitely suppress or repress their own needs and desires. **They differ in that Perfectionists concentrate, often inflexibly, on others' needs based on their own inner standards, while Givers focus on others' needs, often altering themselves in order to make others happy. Although both strive for self-sufficiency and independence, Givers are very relationship oriented and often find themselves overconnected and even indispensable to others.**

L Types One and Three. Perfectionists and Performers can be considered look-alike types because they are both achievers. Both can be goal oriented and success oriented. **The differences are that Perfectionists are more likely to be hounded by their inner critic, which motivates them to do what is judged right by the high standards of the critic, while Performers are more driven to succeed and to change their approach, even cutting corners if necessary, to get to the goal and be recognized for their accomplishments.**

ⓢ Types One and Four. Perfectionists and Romantics share some personality traits because the Perfectionist is the security type of the Romantic and the Romantic is the stress type of the Perfectionist. Both often express idealism, intensity, sensitivity, integrity, authenticity, self-reproach, and a concern for self-improvement. Perfectionists in stress become discouraged and feel deficient. Romantics in security can express a critical idealism and demand perfection or exactness. **They differ in that Perfectionists' idealism concerns correct behavior and "getting it right," while Romantics' idealism revolves around possibilities for ultimate fulfillment. Furthermore, Perfectionists generally are self-restrained, suppressing personal desires, while Romantics experience strong longings and desires, sometimes to the point of self-absorption.**

ⓛ Types One and Five. Perfectionists and Observers can be considered look-alike types because they both are intellectual and can become retracted or internalized when trying to figure things out. **Perfectionists, however, are quite intense, suppress their desires, and seek to improve themselves and others, while Observers detach from feelings in order to protect themselves from being intruded upon and to conserve energy.**

ⓛ Types One and Six. Perfectionists and Loyal Skeptics can be considered look-alike types because both types can be very watchful, anxious and worried, and intent on figuring things out. **What discriminates these two look-alike types is that Loyal Skeptics, by doubting, try to figure out what could go wrong, what the worst-case scenario might be, and how to gain a sense of safety and certainty. Perfectionists, by judging and comparing, try to figure out how to prevent mistakes, how to correct what is wrong, and how to avoid self-criticism and criticism from others.**

⑤ Types One and Seven. Perfectionists and Epicures possess some traits in common because the Perfectionist is the stress type of the Epicure and the Epicure is the security type of the Perfectionist. Both are idealists who want a better world, who show intensity and helpfulness, and who value self-reliance. Perfectionists in security often release themselves from their feelings of responsibility, relaxing into pleasure, personal desire, and playfulness. Epicures in stress can become quite critical, exacting, and determined. **However, while Perfectionists do not seek pleasure and are quite austere, Epicures definitely do seek pleasure and are even hedonistic. Thus, Perfectionists are serious and self-restrained and limit their desires. In contrast, Epicures are fun loving and expansive and spurn limits.**

① Types One and Eight. Perfectionists and Protectors can be considered look-alike types because both are Body Center types (see pages 76–77) and are concerned with rightness, justice, truth, and fairness. **Protectors, however, state their truth openly, express their anger directly, and go from impulse to action easily. Perfectionists suppress anger and impulse, becoming resentful and tense until a sense of righteousness allows their anger to spill out.**

Ⓦ Types One and Nine. Perfectionists and Mediators look alike because as wings of each other and as Body Center types (see pages 76–77) they share some of the same personality traits. They easily forget or suppress their own needs and desires. They value steadiness, organization, and routine, and they work hard for others with care and a concern for harmony. **However, Perfectionists hold to their positions and standards, often rigidly, wanting others to change, while Mediators readily adapt and accommodate to others' positions, often losing sight of their own. Thus, Perfectionists appear tense and press for change, while Mediators go along with others' agendas, adapting to others' requests and claims.**

(W) Types Two and Three. Givers and Performers look alike because as wings of each other and as Heart Center types (see pages 76–77) they share certain personality traits. Both have active, "doing" energy, and both are oriented toward accomplishment and helping. They are exuberant, practical, and approval seeking and often alter themselves to fit whatever image is required. **What distinguishes these two types is that Givers habitually focus on relationships and on others' feelings and needs, in contrast to Performers, who push aside feelings and habitually focus on tasks and goals and getting recognition for their accomplishments.**

(S) Types Two and Four. Givers and Romantics have some personality traits in common because the Giver is the stress type of the Romantic and the Romantic is the security type of the Giver and both are Heart Center types (see pages 76–77). Both are attuned to feelings. Both are sensitive, relationship oriented, helpful, and emotionally intense. Both have a romantic flare and are concerned with image. Givers in security become more internalized, self-oriented, nostalgic, and uniquely creative. Romantics in stress become more pleasing, outer directed, focused on others, and giving. **They differ in that Givers are more outer directed and other-referencing. Givers focus on others' needs with active energy and alter themselves as necessary to meet others' needs. In contrast, Romantics are more inner directed, self-referencing, and subject to feeling "down." Romantics focus on their own specialness or authenticity and are subject to experiencing feelings of deficiency.**

Ⓛ **Types Two and Five.** Givers and Observers can be considered look-alike types because both types are sensitive to the claims and needs of important others, are quite giving, and do not attend to their own feelings. **However, for Observers the periods of giving and responding to claims made by others are intermittent and punctuated by distinct periods of moving away and disconnecting, in order to recharge and protect personal boundaries. Givers, on the other hand, sustain the giving mode, almost always moving forward to connect with others in order to meet others' needs, often losing their personal boundaries in the process.**

Ⓛ **Types Two and Six.** Givers and Loyal Skeptics can be considered look-alikes because both types can be warm and friendly, anxious, sensitive to others, deferring to what others want or need, and disarming or seductive. (This applies especially to the more phobic, or accommodating, Six.) **However, Givers move forward with active energy, focusing on the needs of important others and often feeling indispensable, while Loyal Skeptics warily hold something back, doubt themselves and others, and spurn indispensability. Loyal Skeptics will please others to gain certainty and security rather than to gain a sense of self-worth. In contrast, Givers' self-identity is invested in giving.**

Ⓛ **Types Two and Seven.** Givers and Epicures can be considered look-alike types because both types are active, upbeat, energetic, charming and seductive, friendly, selective in relationships, and want to be liked. **They differ in that Epicures keep their separateness, orienting primarily to themselves, to what they like, want, and need, while Givers move toward others, orienting primarily to the likes, wants, and needs of others. Epicures can easily get absorbed in their own intellectual pursuits, in contrast to Givers, who alter to meet the emotional needs of others.**

⑤ Types Two and Eight. Givers and Protectors share some of the same traits because the Giver is the security type of the Protector and the Protector is the stress type of the Giver. Both show active energy, assertiveness, intrusiveness, generosity, protectiveness toward others, and attraction to power. Givers in stress become more direct and forceful, readily expressing anger and determined that they know what is needed. Protectors in security can be openhearted, expressing feelings, softness, and sensitivity to others. **However, Givers employ their active energy to move toward others with a strong sensitivity to others' feelings, altering themselves to please others and repressing their own needs. By contrast, Protectors use their energy to act forcefully in a way that often intimidates others, asserting their own position, wants, and needs.**

Ⓛ Types Two and Nine. Givers and Mediators can be considered look-alike types because they share the characteristic of pleasing others and meeting others' wants and needs. In the process they orient toward the claims made upon them by others, losing awareness of their own needs and priorities. **The main differences are that Givers more *actively* focus their attention and energy on what others need and alter themselves to meet those needs, while Mediators are more *reactive*, allowing themselves to be pulled by whatever claims are made upon them. They blend in and disperse their energy to make things comfortable without changing their image.**

W **Types Three and Four.** Performers and Romantics look alike because as wings of each other and as Heart Center types (see pages 76–77) they share some personality traits in common. Both have a concern for approval and recognition, and both feel it is important to maintain their image. Both are intense and competitive and have a creative, inventive orientation. **They differ in that Performers sustain a go-ahead goal orientation, which requires them to suspend their feelings and alter themselves, while Romantics have difficulty sustaining a goal orientation because of their fluctuating and deep feelings brought on by their preoccupation with relationships.**

L **Types Three and Five.** Performers and Observers can be considered look-alike types because both types can be oriented toward tasks, activities, and getting things done, and at the same time both detach from their feelings or suspend their feelings so as not to be overly influenced by them. **However, Observers are highly mental and are active and energetic in bursts, interspersed with distinct periods of retraction—time spent recharging and thinking things over. For Performers, activity is much more continuous. Performers will "keep on trucking" with go-ahead energy and concern for presenting a good image.**

S **Types Three and Six.** Performers and Loyal Skeptics share some of the same personality traits because the Performer is the stress type of the Loyal Skeptic and the Loyal Skeptic the security type of the Performer. Both types are personable, practical, highly active, and hardworking. Performers in security are more questioning, reflective, and trusting in others to get things done. Loyal Skeptics in stress move into action, get concerned with their image, and press to get goals accomplished. **They differ in that Loyal Skeptics need to get mobilized for action, overcoming perceived pitfalls and doubts, while Performers sustain a goal orientation with their active, go-ahead energy. Performers thrive on success, compliments, and recognition, in contrast to Loyal Skeptics, who are uncomfortable with these and doubt them.**

ⓛ Types Three and Seven. Performers and Epicures can be considered look-alike types because both types are active, assertive, upbeat, task oriented, activity oriented, and often overbooked. Both tend to avoid negative feelings. **They differ in that Epicures naturally focus on their own pleasures and interests and experience a sense of personal entitlement, especially to keep their options open, whereas Performers are driven to succeed because they need to maintain their good image and get external approval for what they accomplish, in order to sustain their self-worth.**

ⓛ Types Three and Eight. Performers and Protectors can be considered look-alike types because both are assertive, determined, action and goal oriented, and willing to take charge. They also can radiate competence and confidence and may inadvertently step on anyone who gets in their way. **However, Performers will shift gears, alter themselves, and change direction somewhat like chameleons in order to get goals accomplished, while Protectors will hold to a position, get confrontational, and express anger directly and easily. Performers' anger mostly comes up when they feel obstructed in getting to a goal.**

ⓢ Types Three and Nine. Performers and Mediators possess some personality traits in common because the Performer is the security type of the Mediator and the Mediator is the stress type of the Performer. Both types are personable, practical, amiable (wanting to be liked), and competent, and they depend on external support and approval. Performers in stress are more likely to get diverted into secondary tasks and put aside their personal agendas and image. Mediators in security become more singularly focused on their own goals, more efficient, and more image oriented. **What distinguishes them from each other is that Performers are fast paced, efficient, focused on achieving goals, and impatient when obstacles get in their way. On the other hand, Mediators are slower paced, react to the opinions and claims made on them by others, and substitute others' agendas and goals for their own.**

ⓦ Types Four and Five. Romantics and Observers look alike because as wings of each other, they share some of the same personality traits. Both can be analytical, introspective, internalized, sensitive, and shy (yet appear superior). Depending on how much they are influenced by their wings, some Romantics will appear more detached and some Observers more in touch with their feelings. **However, Romantics are the most feeling and emotional type—wanting more from others and having difficulty keeping their personal boundaries. In contrast, Observers are the most detached type—wanting less and keeping more self-contained with clearer personal boundaries.**

ⓛ Types Four and Six. Romantics and counterphobic Loyal Skeptics can be considered look-alike types because both types tend to be contrary, question situations and magnify them, oppose authority, get reckless, break rules, defy dangers, and have periods of self-doubt. **While Loyal Skeptics don't want to become trapped in feelings or longings, Romantics are attracted to feelings and longings. Romantics get expansive and want to be affected emotionally. Furthermore, Loyal Skeptics look for what might go wrong in order to avert or challenge it, while Romantics look for what is missing that could be fulfilling.**

ⓛ Types Four and Seven. Romantics and Epicures can be considered look-alike types because they are both intense and idealistic and want life to be adventuresome and highly stimulating. They both approach life with their attention going to what they want, think, and feel. **However, Epicures are the most upbeat and pleasure-seeking type, avoiding pain and negative feelings whenever possible, while Romantics are just the opposite. They tend to go into melancholy and deep feelings, and they accept pain as part of life.**

Ⓛ Types Four and Eight. Romantics and Protectors can be considered look-alike types because both show intensity, depth and directness of expression (even flamboyance), a lot of energy or emotion, a desire for authenticity, and tendencies toward recklessness, impulsivity, and opposition. **Romantics go deeply into their feelings, often causing them to fall into inaction and lose direction, whereas Protectors surmount their feelings and sustain action with considerable energy.**

Ⓛ Types Four and Nine. Romantics and Mediators can be considered look-alike types because they are both relationship oriented, caring, and empathic. Both can get lost or absorbed in their circumstances, feel deficient, become self-deprecating, and lose their impetus for action. **They differ in that Mediators orient toward others, blend in, and like to keep life steady in order to feel comfortable and avoid conflict. Romantics, by contrast, orient toward themselves, are attached to being special or extraordinary, and readily go to extremes or depths of emotions in order to feel vital and alive.**

Ⓦ Types Five and Six. Observers and Loyal Skeptics look alike because as wings of each other and as Head Center types (see pages 76–77), they share some of the same personality traits. Both can be analytical, reflective, thoughtful, hesitant to take action, and retracted (especially the more phobic Six). **They differ in that Observers detach from or dampen their feelings, compartmentalize circumstances, and usually delay their responses, while Loyal Skeptics react immediately to circumstances, often intensely and with fear, and they magnify the danger of the circumstances to which they are reacting.**

ⓢ Types Five and Seven. Observers and Epicures share some personality traits because the Observer is the security type of the Epicure and the Epicure is the stress type of the Observer and both are Head Center types (see pages 76–77). Both are self-reliant, knowledgeable, and inventive, and love ideas. Both avoid painful feelings. Observers in stress become more externalized, social, active, and oriented toward possibilities. Epicures in security become more internalized, solitary, observant, and inwardly oriented. **They differ in that Observers avoid strong feelings, contain their desires and needs, simplify life, and retract to protect their boundaries. Epicures, on the other hand, actively seek positives, express their desires and needs, get expansive and overbooked, and spurn boundaries and limits.**

ⓢ Types Five and Eight. Observers and Protectors share some of the same personality traits because the Observer is the stress type of the Protector and the Protector is the security type of the Observer. Both types value respect and truth, resist control, become possessive of space and of key resources, and are curious. Observers in security become more engaged and outgoing, and express their desires, their feelings, and their anger. Protectors in stress become more retracted, restrained, and reflective. **However, in general, Observers are the most retracted, contained, and measured type on the Enneagram, conserving their energy, reducing their needs, and almost always thinking before acting. Protectors, by contrast, are the most expansive, expressive, and excessive type on the Enneagram—expanding energy, directly expressing their desires and their anger, and often acting before thinking.**

Ⓛ **Types Five and Nine.** Observers and Mediators can be considered look-alike types because both types can be retracted and introverted, thoughtful, unobtrusive, and even seem to be invisible. Both can withdraw or pull back from being overly influenced by their surroundings. **They differ in that Observers habitually detach from others and assert their boundaries in self-protection, whereas Mediators are the least able to detach from others; they habitually blend with others and go along with others to keep life harmonious and comfortable.**

Ⓦ **Types Six and Seven.** Loyal Skeptics and Epicures look alike because as wings of each other and as Head Center types (see pages 76–77) they share some of the same personality traits. Both are mentally quick, often sharp witted, analytical, imaginative, and able to interrelate diverse ideas. **Loyal Skeptics put a negative spin on experiences, seeing worst-case possibilities and pitfalls, while Epicures put a positive spin on their experiences, planning for multiple positive possibilities. Loyal Skeptics welcome reassuring limits and seek to gain certainty. Epicures abhor limits and seek to expand their options. For Loyal Skeptics pleasure and personal wants are secondary concerns, but for Epicures they are primary.**

Ⓛ **Types Six and Eight.** Counterphobic Loyal Skeptics and Protectors can be considered look-alike types because both can be aggressive, challenging, and confrontive. Both can seem fearless, and both fight for causes. Both share a view of the world as unfriendly and untrustworthy. **Differences arise, however, in how the two types take action. Loyal Skeptics will usually have moments of fear or hesitation before taking action, magnifying the dangers and sometimes giving way under pressure as doubts and questions arise. By contrast, Protectors will react from instinct, taking action without hesitation, minimizing or denying dangers, and holding their ground while denying their vulnerability.**

Ⓢ Types Six and Nine. Loyal Skeptics and Mediators have some personality traits in common because the Loyal Skeptic is the stress type of the Mediator and the Mediator is the security type of the Loyal Skeptic. Both Mediators and the more phobic Loyal Skeptics can be agreeable, accommodating, friendly, anxious to please, self-effacing, sensitive, and eager to avoid conflict. Loyal Skeptics in security are more at ease, relaxed, and accepting of life as it is. Mediators in stress become fearful, questioning, and wary. **However, Loyal Skeptics keep some personal distance, referencing to danger and what could go wrong, while Mediators, the most other-referencing type, often lose themselves in the requests and claims made upon them by others. Mediators go along with others before testing and questioning, whereas Loyal Skeptics test and question before going along with others.**

Ⓦ Types Seven and Eight. Epicures and Protectors look alike because as wings of each other they share certain personality traits. Both are self-assertive, express their wants and desires, believe in their own power and ability, resist limits and controls, and are pleasure oriented. Both have high energy and little inner restraining force. **Epicures avoid pain, explain away or rationalize difficulties, escape conflicts, and go into future planning. Protectors, however, accept pain, engage in difficulties, confront conflicts directly, and live mostly in the present.**

Ⓛ Types Seven and Nine. Epicures and Mediators can be considered look-alike types because both want life to be pleasant and upbeat. They want to be liked and to get along with others. They both avoid conflict. **However, Epicures are more frenetic and fast paced, while Mediators are more even tempered and slower paced. Epicures definitely orient toward themselves, knowing and expressing their own wants, agendas, and opinions. In contrast, Mediators orient toward others, forgetting or deferring their own wants, agendas, and opinions.**

Ⓦ Types Eight and Nine. Protectors and Mediators look alike because as wings of each other and as Body Center types (see pages 76–77) they share some personality traits. Both enjoy earthy pleasures, respond with gut reactions, seek comfort, and are friendly and steadfast. Both get diverted from essential priorities. **The key differences are that Protectors welcome conflict and even anger, while Mediators avoid these. Protectors reference to their own opinions, expressing and defending their opinions as fact. They are decisive. By contrast, Mediators reference to others' opinions and views, losing their own positions in deferring to others. They are often indecisive and go along with others to get along.**

How to Confirm and Verify Your Type

Confirming Your Type for Yourself

When you have reached a tentative decision about the personality type that fits you, consider using the following questions to confirm your decision:

1. When I am under stress or when I mobilize for action, do I shift into some aspects of the stress type connected with the type I believe to be my correct personality type?
2. When I feel relaxed and secure or when I feel *overwhelming* stress, do I shift into some aspects of the security type connected with the type I believe to be my correct personality type?
3. Do I exhibit some of the features of one or both of the wings connected with the type I believe to be my correct personality type?

Verifying Your Type

Once you have discovered and confirmed the personality type that you believe best fits you, you should consider asking someone who knows you well to objectively verify your personality type. Have that person use the Essential Enneagram Test as well as the Type Description pages to review the personality type you chose and to review the alternative types you considered.

If you would like to learn more about the Enneagram, please see appendix A, "Additional Enneagram Resources."

How to Build Self-Understanding

Value of Self-Observation in Discovering Your Type

Ultimately, you discover your Enneagram personality type and facilitate your personal development by observing how your mind works, what your heart feels, and what your body experiences. To develop self-awareness and self-understanding requires a good self-observer. Self-observation practices are essential to the process of personal and professional development and to the management of personality. Just as physical well-being, fitness, and performance depend upon regular exercise, so mental well-being, fitness, and performance depend upon practicing regular self-observation.

A crucial way to develop your ability to observe yourself is to learn and practice the breathing and centering exercise in Section 2. This is the basic exercise for noticing where your attention goes and what thoughts, feelings, and physical sensations you experience. By practicing it, you can discover your habitual patterns and preoccupations. Observing these will greatly help you discover your Enneagram personality type because these patterns and preoccupations are what distinguish one personality from another. As you develop the skill of observing how you habitually use your attention, you can learn to direct your attention to where you really want it to go. Self-observation skills are fundamental to developing conscious awareness and conscious conduct. Developing these skills gives all of us the ability to see ourselves and others more clearly and kindly.

Section 2:
What to Do When You Have
Discovered Your Type

Introduction

This section is divided into two main parts. All of the information and exercises in the first part apply equally to all nine Enneagram personality types. Part 1 begins with a breathing and centering exercise. We then describe five general Enneagram principles that will aid you in understanding yourself. Finally, we discuss nine important elements involved in personal and professional development.

Part 2 offers a series of suggested practices that are specific to each personality type. Each practice is tailored to a particular type and provides practical means for pursuing self-development.

Part 1: General Practices and Principles for All Types

The following breathing and centering practice is referred to throughout the rest of this section. It is a key tool that can help you as you undertake the suggested practices for personal and professional development.

Breathing and Centering

This practice is designed to direct your attention inward, to quiet your mind, and to focus your attention. If you wish, you can tape the steps below and then listen to them as you practice. You can practice these steps for a few minutes or for as long as you like. In the beginning, ten to twenty minutes is optimal. Of course, you can do a breathing practice whenever you need to reduce your reactivity and recenter yourself. When you use the breathing exercise for the practices described later in this section, we suggest you do it for only a few moments.

Steps to Take

1. Sit in a chair with your legs uncrossed and your feet flat on the floor. Close your eyes to help remove your attention from your external surroundings.
2. Put your attention on your breath, and concentrate on it as you breathe in and out. Let your mental state be receptive. Follow your breath, and let your body relax as you breathe. Your breath is a good internal reference point, because it is always there, every moment. And your breath provides a neutral focus, because it has no content or agenda of its own.
3. As you follow your breath in and down, let your breath deepen until it seems to disappear, right into the gravitational center of your body. In this place of grounding deep inside, you have a solid base from which to open your heart and be receptive to yourself and others.
4. When your attention shifts away from your breathing to some thought, feeling, or sensation, just notice it happening. Then let your attention return to your breath. As you continue to follow your breath, you will gradually become free from your ordinary preoccupations and reactions.
5. When you have completed this practice, bring your attention slowly and gently back to your external surroundings. Become aware of yourself sitting in the chair, hear the sounds around you, and open your eyes.

Five General Principles

Below are five general principles related to the Enneagram. Each of the five general principles has three interrelated components. In learning the principles, it may help you to remember that each principle has three parts. Mastering the understanding of these five principles can be very empowering to you as you pursue your personal and professional development.

After reading each principle, take a few minutes to consider ways you could use the principle in your life. Then do the daily practices associated with each of these principles.

Principle I: Three Laws of Behavior

1. Wherever your attention goes, your energy follows, rising and falling with the demands of the situation.
2. Managing your attention and energy requires self-observation. The skill of self-observation is essential in order to be able to alter your attention and your energy as desired and, consequently, your behavior, too.
3. Although self-observation becomes easier as you practice it, it never becomes habitual. Self-observation requires continuing practice.

You can observe for yourself that these three laws of behavior are correct. These laws are central to managing your personality and are fundamental to giving your personal and work life more meaning and fulfillment. The limiting nature of unmanaged habitual personality reactions often leads to conflict, to suffering, and even to failure in both your personal and professional relationships.

Practice Using the Three Laws of Behavior
On the days you do this practice, take a few minutes at the end of the day to review the following questions. Record your responses in a journal, if you like.

- How did I do today at staying aware of where my attention and energy were focused?
- When I reacted automatically to someone or something, was I able to bring back my awareness and redirect my attention and energy?

- How can I practice managing my attention and energy tomorrow?

Principle II: Three Centers of Intelligence

In Western psychology and education the mind has been elevated to prominence as "the" center of intelligence. Yet there is also an intelligence of the heart (emotional intelligence) and an intelligence of the body (sensations and instincts). All three of these intelligences—mind, heart, and body—require ongoing cultivation. Recognizing, developing, and valuing all three centers of intelligence are crucial to all of us in reaching a fulfilling life.

In the Enneagram, the inner triangle of types (Three, Six, and Nine) are the core types of these three centers of intelligence. Each core type has two adjacent types, or wings, that represent variations on the respective core type. Each core type and its two wings constitute a triad. While all types rely to some degree on all three centers of intelligence, each of the types relies heavily on one of the centers—the heart, the mind, or the body, depending on which triad the type is in. This means, for example, that if your type is in the mental triad (Five, Six, Seven) you rely more on the Mind Center of intelligence to guide you than on the Heart Center of intelligence or the Body Center of intelligence.

1. *Heart Center.* If you are a Heart Center type—Two, Three, or Four—you tend to perceive the world through the filter of emotional intelligence. You are attuned to the mood and feeling state in others, in order to maintain your feeling of connection with them. You depend more than other types upon the approval and recognition of others to support your self-esteem and your feeling of being loved. To assure that you get that approval and recognition, you create an image of yourself that will get others to accept you and see you as special. Of course, not only the Heart Center types but all types depend on emotional intelligence to develop the higher qualities of the Heart Center, such as empathy, understanding, compassion, and loving-kindness.

2. *Head Center.* If you are a Head Center type—Five, Six, or Seven—you tend to filter the world through the mental faculties. The goals of this strategy are to minimize anxiety, to manage potentially painful situations, and to gain a sense of certainty through the mental processes of analyzing, envisioning, imagining, and planning. Of course, not only the Head Center types but all types depend upon mental intelligence to develop the higher qualities of the Head Center, such as wisdom, knowing, intuition, and thoughtfulness.

3. *Body Center.* If you are a Body Center type—Eight, Nine, or One—you tend to filter the world through an intelligence of kinesthetic and physical sensations and gut instinct. You use personal position and power to make life be the way you sense it should be. You devise strategies that assure your place in the world and minimize discomfort. Of course, not only the Body Center types but all types depend upon the Body Center of intelligence to be in touch with the energy needed for action, to discern how much power to use in situations, and to supply a sense of being grounded in the world.

Practice Using the Three Centers of Intelligence

On the days you do this practice, take a few minutes at the end of the day to reflect on the following questions. Record your responses in a journal, if you like.

- Given my primary center of intelligence, how did I cultivate all three centers of intelligence today?
- In what ways did I exemplify the higher qualities of each center of intelligence today?
- Based on my reflection, what higher qualities do I need to cultivate tomorrow?

Principle III: Three Life Forces

Knowingly or unknowingly, we all operate from three life forces all the time, and all of them are inherent within us.

1. *Active Force.* The active force provides the energy for action and expression. All that you do and accomplish in the material world uses the active force. The active force gives expression to your thoughts, feelings, and imagination. Western cultures especially value this force. Sometimes the active force is referred to as the creative, affirming, or positive force, because it makes things happen.

2. *Receptive Force.* The receptive force takes in, processes, and digests all the stimuli received by your senses. It is vital to understanding and appreciating the world you live in, to communicating effectively, and to taking right action. Western cultures tend to subordinate the receptive force to the active force and even to devalue it. The receptive force is sometimes referred to as the understanding force, because it takes in and digests impressions. It is also referred to as the negative force, because it counters or reacts to the active force. Yet the receptive force is prerequisite to the third force—the reconciling force.

3. *Reconciling Force.* The reconciling force is the force of consciousness or awareness. It brings your active and receptive forces into correct proportion, into balance and harmony. In this sense, the reconciling force is the master force that you need to develop in order to carry out right action. The reconciling force is sometimes referred to as the preserving, neutralizing, or neutral force, because it has no position per se but balances the other two forces and ultimately sustains you.

The serenity prayer expresses the central role of these three life forces:

God grant me the courage to change the things that I can change (active force), the serenity to accept the things that I cannot change (receptive force), and the wisdom to know the difference (reconciling force).

Mastering these three forces requires recognizing them and understanding how they interact. You need to use your continuing effort every day to bring the active force and the receptive force into awareness and balance.

Practice Balancing the Three Life Forces

On the days you do this practice, take a few minutes at the beginning of the day to become quiet and centered by doing the breathing practice for a few moments. Then repeat to yourself one of these two statements:

> Today I will practice being receptive to the communications of others and aware of my own inner experience as a guide to my actions.

> Today I will practice being aware of my active force and my receptive force and work at balancing them.

Periodically throughout the day, reflect on the statement you chose to repeat to yourself. We suggest you alternate between these two statements from day to day.

Principle IV: Three Survival Behaviors: The Personality Subtypes

Human evolution requires three basic survival behaviors, referred to in the Enneagram as subtypes: the self-preservation subtype, the social, or group, subtype, and the one-to-one, or intimate, subtype. Because these are survival behaviors, each Enneagram personality type includes all three subtypes. Although you manifest all three subtypes to some degree, you usually express one of these three subtypes more than the other two.

1. *Self-Preservation Subtype.* Your attention and energy go to issues related to personal survival, such as safety, security, comfort, protection, and adequate basic resources.
2. *Social Subtype.* Your attention and energy go to issues related to your community and group membership, such as role, status, social acceptance, belonging, participation, and fellowship.
3. *One-to-One Subtype.* Your attention and energy go to issues related to intimate relationships, such as bonding with special others, sexual intimacy, attractiveness, closeness, union, and merging.

It is important to become aware of these three subtypes operating in your life and how they often drive your behavior. One goal of this awareness is to balance your own subtype preoccupations appropriately so that none dominates your life. Another goal of this awareness is to be able to accept differences between you and others. Without the awareness of the influence of these subtype preoccupations, you can experience an imbalance in what your energy is devoted to, and you can experience misunderstandings and conflict with others whose preoccupation differs from yours.

Practice Developing Subtype Awareness

On the days you do this practice, set aside a few minutes to reflect on the following questions about subtype behaviors. Remember that all three subtype behaviors are present in our lives. Record your responses in a journal, if you like.

- How do the self-preservation, social, and one-to-one subtypes manifest themselves in my life, and which one tends to dominate?
- How does my subtype preoccupation cause difficulty in my relationships, and how does it benefit them?
- What do I need to do, or stop doing, to bring balance into my life with respect to the subtypes?

Principle V: Three Levels of Knowing and Learning

We all have three interrelated ways of knowing and learning, and it is useful to be able to distinguish among them. Although the higher levels are more advanced and require more skill, each way has value.

1. *Knowing Based on Your Habit of Mind: Incremental Learning.* This level of knowing and learning is based on your personality type and is determined largely by the core beliefs and the attentional style of your type. This level of learning occurs almost automatically through the five senses. It requires little personal awareness because it is based on the habitual thoughts, feelings,

and sensations of your type. Once you have identified your personality type, you can use a number of different strategies to promote your personal growth. See the Personal Development section of the Type Description pages for a list of these strategies.

2. *Knowing Based on Conscious Awareness: Reconstructive Learning.* This level of knowing and learning requires you to consciously observe your thoughts, feelings, and sensations. Maintaining awareness of the biases generated by your type's core beliefs, coping strategy, and attentional style gives you choice. This level of knowing involves questioning and reflecting on your usual assumptions and replacing your automatic reactions with consciously and deliberately made choices. To work at this level of knowing and learning, you need to internalize both the material on the Type Description pages and the general and specific practices in this section of the book.

3. *Direct Knowing: Transformational Learning.* The third level of knowing and learning harnesses the specific energy of your type and uses it as a transforming agent to transcend your type and its core beliefs, strategy, and attentional style. Direct knowing is based on a level of awareness that allows action to precede, not follow, the usual thoughts, feelings, and sensations of your type. Direct knowing, or transformational learning, requires you to be willing to experience your life from a perspective that is not based on a fixed position or identity. It requires you to take an openly receptive stance, where personality biases drop away. From this stance, your intellectual curiosity and emotional openness enable you to experience life directly without the distortion or bias of your type. The Enneagram provides you with specific ways to pursue this work of transformation. To master this level of knowing and learning is a lifelong endeavor and entirely voluntary. "The ultimate goal of my development" in the Type Description pages as well as the reflection practices in this section provide an overview of the transformation tasks.

Elements of Personal and Professional Development: The Nine Cs

Begin the work of personal and professional development by centering yourself, in order to be able to practice self-observation. Become consciously aware of how your energy follows your habitual placement of attention, what your current preoccupations are, and how your behavior flows from these. Use this awareness to learn to contain your energy rather than discharge it into habitual patterns. Learn to convert your energy into conscious conduct.

The nine Cs described below are central to the efficient and effective work of personal and professional development, to wholeness, and to well-being.

1. *Center Yourself.* Center yourself by practicing the breathing exercise for a few moments.
2. *Cultivate Your Consciousness.* Cultivate consciousness in yourself by using self-observation to discover what your current preoccupations are.
3. *Collect Your Energy.* Collect your energy back into yourself, into the gravitational center of your body, when it wants to discharge into habitual reactions.
4. *Contain Your Energy.* Contain your energy by concentrating your attention on experiencing your feelings instead of discharging your energy in a habitual, type-determined way. Resist the urge to take immediate action.
5. *Consider the Meaning of Your Usual Reaction.* Consider what your usual automatic response is about by using inner inquiry and self-reflection.
6. *Convert Your Energy to Conscious Conduct.* Convert your habitual responses into conscious conduct by using your awareness to coach and encourage yourself to try healthier courses of action.
7. *Compassion.* Manifest compassion by adopting a kind and caring attitude toward yourself and others.

8. *Consequences.* Consider the consequences, or effects, of your conscious conduct by noticing the impact of your behavior on yourself and on others.
9. *Clarity.* Gain clarity about the process of personal and professional development by reflecting upon and internalizing the previous eight elements of development.

You can use this nine-step process regardless of your particular personality type simply by focusing on the issues and dilemmas associated with your type. When you have difficulty with a particular step, put more attention into mastering that step.

Part 2: Specific Practices for Each Type

For each of the nine personality types, you will find four specific practices. These practices provide you with opportunities to become more aware of how your personality functions, to take action to change your habitual behavior, to preview and review your progress in self-development, and to reflect on the ultimate goal of your development.

Practice Awareness. This practice builds your self-observer and focuses on a key aspect of your type.

Practice Taking Action. This practice focuses on changing an habitual behavior associated with your type.

Practice Previewing and Reviewing Your Progress. This practice gives you the opportunity to work on the central issue of your type. This is perhaps the most important practice for personal and professional development.

Practice Reflecting. This practice leads you to reclaim the fundamental principle associated with your type and to pursue the ultimate task of self-development of your type.

Practices for the Perfectionist (Type One)

We recommend that you begin by choosing just one practice to work on before you move on to the others. It may take you a week or more with each practice to experience a sense of progress. You might find it helpful to keep a journal to record your daily responses to these practices.

Practice Awareness

Pay particular attention to the dominance of your inner critic and its incessant demands. Stop several times a day for a minute or so to consider the following questions:

How have I been judging myself and others? How constantly present has the voice of judgment been? How has my inner critic made me feel? In what ways has my inner critic been affecting my behavior?

Practice Taking Action

Recall that Perfectionists tend to be dominated by the dictates of their inner critic to always do what is correct and responsible. Consequently, they end up suppressing their personal needs and their natural desires for pleasure.

So, each day consciously and deliberately include time for personal needs, natural desires, and pleasurable activities (at least some of which have nothing to do with self-improvement per se). Schedule inviolate time for these activities.

Notice when internal resistance comes up to doing enjoyable things. Use this resistance as a signal to go ahead and do them.

To check the value of this practice for you, notice if you are experiencing more balance of work and pleasure in your life. Remember that Perfectionists can get so driven by responsibility and by doing work before pleasure that they never get to the pleasure.

Practice Previewing and Reviewing Your Progress

Preview:

When you first get up in the morning, center yourself by practicing the breathing exercise for a few moments. Then say to yourself,

Today I will practice accepting my own and others' mistakes and errors as part of the natural flow of life. I will practice appreciating different points of view, different values, and different ways of doing things. I can do this by releasing resentments when they arise and practicing forgiveness. I will try to bring a sense of harmony and balance between work and pleasure into my life today.

When you do this practice, adopt the stance that the changes you are previewing are already true about you.

Review:
In the evening, take a few minutes to review your progress today. Ask yourself with an open mind and heart,

How did I do today at accepting mistakes and errors? At appreciating differences? At forgiving? At experiencing a sense of harmony and balance between work and pleasure?

Use what you learn from this review to guide your thoughts and actions for tomorrow.

Practice Reflecting
At least once a week, take a few minutes in a quiet place to reflect upon and contemplate both the fundamental principle and the ultimate task for Perfectionists. A natural outdoor setting is an ideal place to do this.

The *fundamental principle* Perfectionists lose sight of and need to regain is that we are all one and we are perfect as we are. Therefore, the *ultimate task* for Perfectionists is to reclaim perfection by regaining a sense that life is good as it is, not divided into right and wrong as Perfectionists perceive it to be. This ultimate task is more easily accomplished when you accept differences and mistakes, experience compassion and forgiveness toward yourself and others, and allow yourself time to relax and enjoy life.

Then explore what adopting these truths would mean to your life.

Practices for the Giver (Type Two)

We recommend that you begin by choosing just one practice to work on before you move on to the others. It may take you a week or more with each practice to experience a sense of progress. You might find it helpful to keep a journal to record your daily responses to these practices.

Practice Awareness

Pay particular attention to how much your attention and energy go to others' needs and feelings. Stop several times a day for a minute or so to consider the following questions:

> How much of my attention and energy have gone into responding to others' wants, needs, and feelings? How much of my time has been absorbed by others' needs? What have I done when I've seen that someone or something needs my help? In what ways have I been adapting myself to meet others' expectations?

Practice Taking Action

Recall that Givers tend to believe they must fulfill others' needs in order to gain approval and love.

So, each day make a conscious effort to ask yourself what you want and need from both yourself and others. Deliberately make your own wants and needs primary.

Notice when a feeling of selfishness or guilt comes up to try to stop you from taking care of yourself or from asking for what you need from others. If you notice a rising emotional intensity in yourself, use this feeling as a clue that you are not paying sufficient attention to your own wants and needs.

To check the value of this practice for you, notice if you are really feeling nurtured. Remember that Givers have a powerful tendency to repress their own needs and become absorbed in fulfilling others' needs.

Practice Previewing and Reviewing Your Progress

Preview:
When you first get up in the morning, center yourself by practicing the breathing exercise for a few moments. Then say to yourself,

Today I will practice giving and receiving equally, as my own needs and others' needs become apparent to me. I will practice doing this with an open and generous heart. I can do this by taking time to develop my own independence and autonomy, by nurturing my own interests, and by looking out for my own well-being as conscientiously as I look out for the interests and well-being of others.

When you do this practice, adopt the stance that the changes you are previewing are already true about you.

Review:
In the evening, take a few minutes to review your progress today. Ask yourself with an open mind and heart,

How did I do today in giving and receiving equally? How was I in being open and generous toward myself as well as others? Did I take time to fulfill my own interests and needs?

Use what you learn from this review to guide your thoughts and actions for tomorrow.

Practice Reflecting
At least once a week, take a few minutes in a quiet place to reflect upon and contemplate both the fundamental principle and the ultimate task for Givers. A natural outdoor setting is an ideal place to do this.

The *fundamental principle* Givers lose sight of and need to regain is that everyone's needs are equally and freely met. Therefore, the *ultimate task* for Givers is to realize that being loved and receiving approval are not dependent on being needed and don't depend on how much you give to others. This ultimate task is more easily accomplished when you realize that paying attention to your own personal wants and needs and receiving what you want and need from others is as important as taking care of the wants and needs of others.

Then explore what adopting these truths would mean to your life.

Practices for the Performer (Type Three)

We recommend that you begin by choosing just one practice to work on before you move on to the others. It may take you a week or more with each practice to experience a sense of progress. You might find it helpful to keep a journal to record your daily responses to these practices.

Practice Awareness

Pay particular attention to your feelings and your tendency to put them aside in favor of efficient action. Stop several times a day for a minute or so to consider the following questions:

> What feelings have occurred in me since I last stopped to check? What tasks have I been putting my energy into when these feelings came up? How have I avoided or suspended these feelings?

Practice Taking Action

Recall that Performers often suspend or avoid feelings, because feelings seem to get in the way of efficient action.

So, each day make a conscious effort to moderate your pace at work and in your personal life.

Notice your hard-driving energy, your time urgency and impatience, and your preoccupation with things to do. Knowing that your tendency is to do everything fast, stop yourself for a few moments, and breathe deeply and slowly. Let your attention follow your breath into the center of your body and away from the demands of the world. Then, in this quieter state, determine to practice a more moderate pace.

To check the value of this practice for you, notice if you are taking the time to be aware of your own feelings and to really listen to others. Remember that Performers can get so focused on multiple goals and achieving results that they screen out their own feelings and what others are trying to communicate to them.

Practice Previewing and Reviewing Your Progress

Preview:

When you first get up in the morning, center yourself by practicing the breathing exercise for a few moments. Then say to yourself,

> Today I will practice knowing that getting things done is not solely dependent upon my own effort and efficiency. I will practice letting go of *constant* doing and become more conscious of what I really *need* to do. I can do this by staying in touch with my feelings and letting them guide me.

When you do this practice, adopt the stance that the changes you are previewing are already true about you.

Review:

In the evening, take a few minutes to review your progress today. Ask yourself with an open mind and heart,

> How did I do today at distinguishing what to let go of and what to accomplish? How receptive was I to my real feelings and to maintaining a pace that was in harmony with my feelings?

Use what you learn from this review to guide your thoughts and actions for tomorrow.

Practice Reflecting

At least once a week, take a few minutes in a quiet place to reflect upon and contemplate both the fundamental principle and the ultimate task for Performers. A natural outdoor setting is an ideal place to do this.

The *fundamental principle* Performers lose sight of and need to regain is that everything works and gets done naturally according to universal laws, not simply by the individual efforts of the doer. Therefore, the *ultimate task* for Performers is to know that recognition and love come from who you are, not from what you do. This ultimate task is more easily accomplished when you accept that constant accomplishment is not what life is about.

Then explore what adopting these truths would mean to your life.

Practices for the Romantic (Type Four)

We recommend that you begin by choosing just one practice to work on before you move on to the others. It may take you a week or more with each practice to experience a sense of progress. You might find it helpful to keep a journal to record your daily responses to these practices.

Practice Awareness

Pay particular attention to how much time you spend missing and longing for things that feel important but are not present in your life. Stop several times a day for a minute or so to consider the following questions:

> What have I been feeling disappointed about? What have I been feeling that there's not enough of in my life? How has what seems special or ideal, but not available, been dominating my attention? What or who have I been experiencing as just fine and not lacking in any way?

Practice Taking Action

Recall that Romantics often get so absorbed in what would be ideal but is lacking that they tend to miss what is positive about the present.

So, each day consciously embrace and appreciate the ordinary experiences of everyday life. Appreciate the little things, such as necessary daily tasks, ordinary encounters with others, and whatever beauty is around you.

If you notice your attention drifting away to what is missing or to feeling disappointed with the way things are, use this experience as a signal to return your attention to the present and to make the ordinary meaningful.

To check the value of this practice for you, notice if you are experiencing the present as more fulfilling and less disappointing. Remember that Romantics, because their attention is absorbed in past and future ideals, often fail to appreciate much of ordinary everyday life.

Practice Previewing and Reviewing Your Progress

Preview:
When you first get up in the morning, center yourself by practicing the breathing exercise for a few moments. Then say to yourself,

> Today I will practice living in emotional balance and sustaining a steady course of action, despite any fluctuating feelings I experience. I can do this by not being swayed by strong emotions or dominated by what is disappointing, and by appreciating what is positive and meaningful in the ordinary flow of life.

When you do this practice, adopt the stance that the changes you are previewing are already true about you.

Review:
In the evening, take a few minutes to review your progress today. Ask yourself with an open mind and heart,

> How did I do today at appreciating what is present and fulfilling in my life rather than lamenting what is absent and disappointing? Did I sustain a steady course of action despite fluctuating feelings? Did I resist getting absorbed in strong feelings of longing or envy? Did I experience more of a sense of wholeness?

Use what you learn from this review to guide your thoughts and actions for tomorrow.

Practice Reflecting

At least once a week, take a few minutes in a quiet place to reflect upon and contemplate both the fundamental principle and the ultimate task for Romantics. A natural outdoor setting is an ideal place to do this.

The *fundamental principle* Romantics lose sight of and need to regain is that everyone has a deep and complete connection to all others and all things. Therefore, the *ultimate task* for Romantics is to realize that a sense of wholeness and love come from appreciating what is already present in the here and now. This ultimate task is more easily accomplished when you realize that feelings of something missing are a consequence of idealizing the past and the future instead of focusing on satisfaction in the present.

Then explore what adopting these truths would mean to your life.

Practices for the Observer (Type Five)

We recommend that you begin by choosing just one practice to work on before you move on to the others. It may take you a week or more with each practice to experience a sense of progress. You might find it helpful to keep a journal to record your daily responses to these practices.

Practice Awareness

Pay particular attention to your tendency to limit your emotional involvement by detaching from your feelings and disengaging from others. Stop several times a day for a minute or so to consider the following questions:

How have I been limiting my emotional involvement? In what ways have I been avoiding my own and others' feelings? When others have expressed their emotions, have I detached and withdrawn into my mind?

Practice Taking Action

Recall that Observers often detach from their feelings and disengage from others because they are concerned that others might intrude upon them and demand too much of them.

So, each day make a conscious effort to practice a sense of abundance. Act from the position that there are ample resources and energy. Give more of yourself and take more from the world around you.

Observe and counter your tendency to withdraw to conserve energy. Notice when you react by retracting, and use that as a signal to stay present and connected.

To check the value of this practice for you, notice if you are staying more attached to your feelings and more engaged with others rather than reverting to your inclination to withdraw. Remember that a sense of abundance seems counter-instinctive to Observers, who are concerned about scarcity and the depletion of energy in a world they believe takes too much and gives too little.

Practice Previewing and Reviewing Your Progress

Preview:
When you first get up in the morning, center yourself by practicing the breathing exercise for a few moments. Then say to yourself,

> Today I will practice staying engaged in what is going on around me. I will practice maintaining my connection to others and to my own feelings. I can do this by observing my tendency to retract and disconnect and by counteracting this tendency.

When you do this practice, adopt the stance that the changes you are previewing are already true about you.

Review:
In the evening, take a few minutes to review your progress today. Ask yourself with an open mind and heart,

> How did I do today at keeping myself engaged in the flow of life? What did I do to stay connected to others and to my feelings? How did I reverse my self protective tendency to retract and withdraw?

Use what you learn from this review to guide your thoughts and actions for tomorrow.

Practice Reflecting

At least once a week, take a few minutes in a quiet place to reflect upon and contemplate both the fundamental principle and the ultimate task for Observers. A natural outdoor setting is an ideal place to do this.

The *fundamental principle* Observers lose sight of and need to regain is that there is an ample supply of all the knowledge and energy everyone needs. Therefore, the *ultimate task* for Observers is to stay engaged in the flow of life, giving and taking freely. This ultimate task is more easily accomplished when you experience the fact that staying connected with your feelings and with others does not deplete you but instead supports you.

Then explore what adopting these truths would mean to your life.

Practices for the Loyal Skeptic (Type Six)

We recommend that you begin by choosing just one practice to work on before you move on to the others. It may take you a week or more with each practice to experience a sense of progress. You might find it helpful to keep a journal to record your daily responses to these practices.

Practice Awareness

Pay particular attention to how much your attention and energy go to worst-case scenarios and to selecting information that supports negative, harmful possibilities. Stop several times a day for a minute or so to consider the following questions:

What harmful or hazardous outcomes have come to my mind? What has felt threatening to me? How have I been watchful, wary, cautious, or challenging? What self-doubts and worst-case scenarios have been preoccupying me?

Practice Taking Action

Recall that Loyal Skeptics tend to doubt and to fear the worst because of a loss of trust in themselves and others.

So, each day make a conscious effort to take appropriate action despite doubt or fear. Face what seem like hazards; don't avoid them (a phobic response) or challenge them (a counterphobic response).

When you feel apprehensive, anxious, or fearful (phobic)—or tense, hyper, or challenging (counterphobic)—center and ground yourself by breathing deeply. Then, move forward into action, reminding yourself that fear does not have to go away before you can act.

To check the value of this practice for you, notice if you are taking appropriate action without having to first dispel fear or excessively test and validate your course of action. Remember that Loyal Skeptics habitually avoid hazards (a phobic response) or challenge them (a counterphobic response). As a way of coping with doubt and fear, Phobic Sixes seek security and Counterphobic Sixes defy security. Flight and fight are both responses to perceived danger.

Practice Previewing and Reviewing Your Progress

Preview:

When you first get up in the morning, center yourself by practicing the breathing exercise for a few moments. Then say to yourself,

> Today I will practice acting with faith in myself and trust in others, just as a person who already has these qualities would act. I can do this by taking action before I have proof or certainty about my course of action and by believing in my own resources and abilities.

When you do this practice, adopt the stance that the changes you are previewing are already true about you.

Review:

In the evening, take a few minutes to review your progress today. Ask yourself with an open mind and heart,

> How did I do today at having faith in myself and having trust in others? In what ways did I move forward into action without having to dispel fear or gain certainty about the course of action? How well did I steady my attention on what is positive?

Use what you learn from this review to guide your thoughts and actions for tomorrow.

Practice Reflecting

At least once a week, take a few minutes in a quiet place to reflect upon and contemplate both the fundamental principle and the ultimate task for Loyal Skeptics. A natural outdoor setting is an ideal place to do this.

The *fundamental principle* Loyal Skeptics lose sight of and need to regain is that we all have faith in ourselves, in others, and in the world. Therefore, the *ultimate task* for Loyal Skeptics is to trust self and others. This ultimate task is more easily accomplished when you notice your doubt or fear and calm it, when you move ahead in spite of lingering doubt or fear, and when you accept uncertainty as a natural part of life.

Then explore what adopting these truths would mean to your life.

Practices for the Epicure (Type Seven)

We recommend that you begin by choosing just one practice to work on before you move on to the others. It may take you a week or more with each practice to experience a sense of progress. You might find it helpful to keep a journal to record your daily responses to these practices.

Practice Awareness

Pay particular attention to how much your attention and energy go to planning for pleasurable, positive possibilities. Stop several times a day for a minute or so to consider the following questions:

How have I been turning my mind to new and interesting activities when faced with something negative? How have I circumvented frustrations? What various options and opportunities have been absorbing my attention and energy?

Practice Taking Action

Recall that Epicures try to avoid fear, pain, and limitations by generating multiple positive options for themselves to pursue. But Epicures actually limit themselves by habitually steering away from everything that could involve fear or pain.

So, each day consciously practice following through on every agreement you have made and on all the responsibilities you have undertaken, despite the pains and frustrations you may experience.

Recognize your tendency to escape what feels limiting or negative. Notice how you come up with good reasons and alternatives for getting out of what you don't want to do. Notice when something (like this practice) starts to seem frustrating and limiting to you. Use that as a signal to "hold your feet to the fire"—to continue what you have started.

To check the value of this practice for you, notice if you are fulfilling your agreements and responsibilities more, particularly the ones you find tedious, frustrating, or unpleasant. Notice how this feels. Remember that Epicures have a strategy of keeping life upbeat and boundless, which makes them susceptible to rationalizing away painful or frustrating responsibilities.

Practice Previewing and Reviewing Your Progress

Preview:
When you first get up in the morning, center yourself by practicing the breathing exercise for a few moments. Then say to yourself,

> Today I will practice keeping my attention and energy in the present moment, no matter what frustrations and painful feelings life presents to me. I will also practice keeping others in mind, and not just my own agenda. I can do this by accepting all of life in the here and now and by staying aware of my tendency to divert my attention and energy into planning for pleasurable options and future opportunities.

When you do this practice, adopt the stance that the changes you are previewing are already true about you.

Review:
In the evening, take a few minutes to review your progress today. Ask yourself with an open mind and heart,

> How did I do today at keeping my attention and energy in the present moment? How did I do at keeping in mind the well-being of others, not just my own well-being? How well did I keep my commitment to doing this practice?

Use what you learn from this review to guide your thoughts and actions for tomorrow.

Practice Reflecting

At least once a week, take a few minutes in a quiet place to reflect upon and contemplate both the fundamental principle and the ultimate task for Epicures. A natural outdoor setting is an ideal place to do this.

The *fundamental principle* Epicures lose sight of and need to regain is that life is a full spectrum of possibilities to be experienced deeply and with sustained concentration. Therefore, the *ultimate task* for Epicures is to accept that a complete life contains a spectrum of joy and sorrow, pleasure and pain, opportunity and limitation. This ultimate task is more easily accomplished when you accept all of life in the present moment, staying grounded in spite of the presence of uncomfortable emotions or tedious tasks.

Then explore what adopting these truths would mean to your life.

Practices for the Protector (Type Eight)

We recommend that you begin by choosing just one practice to work on before you move on to the others. It may take you a week or more with each practice to experience a sense of progress. You might find it helpful to keep a journal to record your daily responses to these practices.

Practice Awareness

Pay particular attention to both the positive and negative impact of your energy on others. Stop several times a day for a minute or so to consider the following questions:

How has my energy and the way I express myself been impacting others? In what ways have I evoked resistance or confrontation? Have I caused anyone to back off from me or withdraw into themselves? How have I been excessive? Too loud? Too invasive?

Practice Taking Action

Recall that Protectors have a big, forceful energy, which is often experienced by others as excessive, or too much, even when Protectors are holding some of it back. Protectors are often simply unaware that the impact they have may be overwhelming to others.

So, each day make a conscious effort to moderate your urge to use direct action to express your desires and your sense of justice and truth.

Notice how the urge to express yourself comes from your gut, from your body. Contain your initial impulse to take direct action while you consider the possible consequences. Ask yourself if a more moderate approach would be better.

To check the value of this practice for you, notice if you are respecting others' boundaries and positions. Remember that Protectors take an all-or-nothing approach to relating to others, which makes it difficult for them to be moderate.

Practice Previewing and Reviewing Your Progress

Preview:
When you first get up in the morning, center yourself by practicing the breathing exercise for a few moments. Then say to yourself:

> Today I will practice coming to each situation more open to others' different positions and different energy. I will practice being more aware and accepting of my own natural vulnerabilities and tender feelings. I can do this by recognizing that my denial of my vulnerability and of my softer feelings is a deeply embedded habit that doesn't serve me well.

When you do this practice, adopt the stance that the changes you are previewing are already true about you.

Review:
In the evening, take a few minutes to review your progress today. Ask yourself with an open mind and heart,

> How did I do today in approaching each situation open to others' different positions and energy? How was I at accepting my own natural vulnerabilities and tender feelings?

Use what you learn from this review to guide your thoughts and actions for tomorrow.

Practice Reflecting

At least once a week, take a few minutes in a quiet place to reflect upon and contemplate both the fundamental principle and the ultimate task for Protectors. A natural outdoor setting is an ideal place to do this.

The *fundamental principle* Protectors lose sight of and need to regain is that we are all innocent and without guile, and we can all sense the truth. Therefore, the *ultimate task* for Protectors is to reclaim the original innocence of coming to each situation without prejudging it or overpowering it and to realize that truth flows from universal laws, not from personal views. This ultimate task is more easily accomplished when you approach each situation with an appropriate energy, or force, and with an equal respect for yourself and others.

Then explore what adopting these truths would mean to your life.

Practices for the Mediator (Type Nine)

We recommend that you begin by choosing just one practice to work on before you move on to the others. It may take you a week or more with each practice to experience a sense of progress. You might find it helpful to keep a journal to record your daily responses to these practices.

Practice Awareness

Pay particular attention to how much your attention and energy gets pulled by and then dispersed into the many claims made upon you, leading to indecisiveness and overaccommodation. Stop several times a day for a minute or so to consider the following questions:

How have all the people and things around me been pulling at and competing for my attention? How indecisive have I been? In what ways have I gone along with others' agendas and plans? In what ways have I been sidetracked into secondary priorities or inessentials?

Practice Taking Action

Recall that Mediators tend to have their attention pulled by everything around them, which allows them to blend in and feel a sense of belonging. This sense of belonging gives Mediators a sense of their importance, which they have forgotten.

So, each day make a conscious effort to place your attention on what is important to you and to use your energy for your own priorities, despite the discomfort or conflict that might arise from doing this.

Notice that discomfort gets experienced as an uneasiness in your gut. Be aware that going along with others' agendas and diverting your attention to small pleasures or secondary tasks reduces the discomfort. Do your best to avoid these coping strategies, to hold your ground, to acknowledge your importance as an individual, and to express yourself accordingly.

To check the value of this practice for you, notice if you are following your own agenda and if that is helping to restore your sense of your importance as an individual. Evaluate how you are facing potential and actual situations of conflict or discomfort. Remember that Mediators tend to avoid conflict and seek comfort as a strategy for coping with the belief that their own priorities and opinions are not important.

Practice Previewing and Reviewing Your Progress

Preview:

When you first get up in the morning, center yourself by practicing the breathing exercise for a few moments. Then say to yourself,

Today I will practice loving myself in a way equal to how I love others. I will practice appreciating my good qualities. When I need to make a decision, I will try to treat my own opinion as being as important as the opinion of others. I can do this by setting my own personal priorities and by respecting my own limits and boundaries.

When you do this practice, adopt the stance that the changes you are previewing are already true about you.

Review:
In the evening, take a few minutes to review your progress today. Ask yourself with an open mind and heart,

In what ways did I express self-love and self-regard today? How did I respect my own limits and boundaries? How did I do in setting and carrying out my own personal priorities? Did I treat myself as equally important as others?

Use what you learn from this review to guide your thoughts and actions for tomorrow.

Practice Reflecting

At least once a week, take a few minutes in a quiet place to reflect upon and contemplate both the fundamental principle and the ultimate task for Mediators. A natural outdoor setting is an ideal place to do this.

The *fundamental principle* Mediators lose sight of and need to regain is that everyone belongs equally in a state of unconditional love and union. Therefore, the *ultimate task* for Mediators is to reclaim unconditional self-love and a sense of importance equal to others. This ultimate task is more easily accomplished when you pay attention to your own position and priorities and when you act in ways that are essential to your own well-being and to the well-being of others.

Then explore what adopting these truths would mean to your life.

Appendix A:
Additional Enneagram Resources

The resources listed here are from the Enneagram in the Oral Tradition of Helen Palmer. Teaching and learning in this tradition involves using the panel interviewing method and the principle of self-discovery. *The Essential Enneagram* is based on this principle of self-discovery. The oral tradition makes it possible for all individuals to speak for themselves as they are to themselves.

Books

The Enneagram: Understanding Yourself and the Others in Your Life by Helen Palmer. San Francisco: HarperSanFrancisco, 1988.

The Enneagram in Love and Work by Helen Palmer. San Francisco: HarperSanFrancisco, 1995.

The Pocket Enneagram by Helen Palmer. San Francisco: HarperSanFrancisco, 1995.

The Enneagram Advantage by Helen Palmer. New York: Harmony Books, 1998.

Healing Your Habit of Mind: Practical Applications of the Enneagram in Daily Life by David Daniels and Helen Palmer. In preparation.

Videos

Helen Palmer:
The Stanford University Panels of the Nine Types (with David Daniels), 1994.
Nine Points of View on Addiction and Recovery, 1994.
Women on Relationship and Men on Relationship, 1994.

Available through:
Helen Palmer
1442A Walnut Street, Suite 377
Berkeley, CA 94709
Phone: (510) 843-7621
E-mail: eptpoffice@aol.com

David N. Daniels, M.D., and Courtney Behm, M.B.A.:
Nine Paths to a Productive and Fulfilling Life: A Comprehensive Overview of the Enneagram, 1999.
The Enneagram in the Workplace: Nine Paths to Effective Leadership and Performance, 2000.

Available through:
CC-M Productions, Inc.
7755 16th Street, N.W.
Washington, D.C. 20012
Phone: (800) 453-6280
Website: www.managementwisdom.com
E-mail: bob@cc-m.com

Audio Tapes

The Enneagram: Eight-Hour Introduction by Helen Palmer
Produced by Sounds True Recordings

Available through Helen Palmer as cited above.
Order also through Sounds True: (800) 333-9185

Organizations

International Enneagram Association
IEA Headquarters
1060 North Fourth Street
San Jose, CA 95112
Phone: (408) 971-5905
Website: www.intl-enneagram-assn.org

Association of Enneagram Teachers in the Oral Tradition
1442A Walnut Street, Suite 377
Berkeley, CA 94709
Phone: (510) 843-7621
Website: ennegramteachers.org

Enneagram Classes

Enneagram Professional and Personal Development Training
    Programs, Workshops, and Seminars
1442A Walnut Street, Suite 377
Berkeley, CA 94709
Phone: (510) 843-7621
E-mail: PalmrDanls@aol.com or drdaniels@batnet.com
Website: www.AuthenticEnneagram.com
    www.enneagram-site.com

Newsletter

Enneagram Monthly
117 Sweetmilk Creek Road
Troy, NY 12180-9105
Phone: (518) 279-4444
E-mail: enneamonth@aol.com

Appendix B:
Validity of the Essential Enneagram Test

We designed a simple paragraph test based on logical constructs of the nine Enneagram personality types derived from the theoretical work of Helen Palmer and David Daniels. Each paragraph includes:

- the overall worldview of the type
- the attentional style
- the dominant mental and emotional biases
- the central preoccupations
- the positive attributes of the type

We asked representatives of each personality type to review and revise their respective paragraphs to ensure that the paragraphs were congruent with their actual experience of being that type. We then reviewed their revisions to ensure that the paragraphs were accurate from a theoretical standpoint and were equally socially desirable.

We established the Essential Enneagram Test's validity by testing 970 individuals throughout the United States who enrolled in Enneagram classes or volunteered for typing interviews. These individuals did not know their Enneagram personality type and were unfamiliar with the Enneagram. Sixty-five percent of the sample were women. Thirty-five percent were men.

We compared each individual's Essential Enneagram Test self-rating to one of two "gold standard" ratings:

- One of the gold standards used was diagnostic typing interviews conducted by certified Enneagram teachers who did not know how the individuals had rated themselves.
- The other gold standard was the individual's own reevaluation on the Assessment Inventory after taking a ten-week Enneagram course or its equivalent.

The two gold standards produced similar results. These results are used to indicate the validity of the Essential Enneagram Test, the probability that users will accurately select their personality type from among the nine paragraphs.

We analyzed the results for each of the nine paragraphs separately. Each of the nine paragraphs, or personality types, has its own probability of accurately discriminating among the nine Enneagram personality types. The Type Determination pages in *The Essential Enneagram* show the validity of each paragraph. For example, the Perfectionist paragraph has a 66 percent validity. This means that two-thirds of the people who selected the Perfectionist paragraph as their type were also identified as this type by the gold standard, either by an expert's rating through a structured interview or by their own reevaluation of themselves following an Enneagram course.

People sometimes choose a paragraph in the Essential Enneagram Test that is not their correct personality type but is one of the look-alike types[1] associated with their personality type or is one of the four personality types connected[2] to their personality type. For this reason, we also calculated the probability of individuals being each of the other eight types, if their self-rating was not correct when compared to the gold standard. The Type Determination pages in *The Essential Enneagram* show these other analyses. For example, 8 percent of the subjects who chose the Perfectionist paragraph are actually Romantics, 8 percent are Loyal Skeptics, 7 percent are Givers, and

---

[1]Look-alike types are the personality types on the Enneagram that bear a similarity to each other.

[2]There are four types associated with each personality type, according to Enneagram personality theory. They are the two wings and the security type and the stress type.

5 percent are Mediators. The remaining 6 percent of those who typed themselves as the Perfectionist are distributed among the remaining four types.

The Type Determination pages include step-by-step instructions for the readers of this book who take the Essential Enneagram test to determine the accuracy of their choices.

We performed the following statistical analyses. We analyzed each paragraph in the Essential Enneagram test with respect to sensitivity, specificity, predictive value of positives, predictive value of negatives, test efficiency, and Cohen's Kappa test for intraclass correlation. We computed Kappa statistics for the test across all nine scales as a measure of overall test concordance. Test validity as measured by congruency of respondents' answers to the gold standard were statistically and clinically significant. The overall Kappa for the entire test was 0.5254 (P <0.0001), considered a significant degree of concordance. All analyses of individual items exhibited concordance or intraclass correlations significant at P <0.0001. We performed reliability analysis with a small naïve group ($n = 62$) of graduate students. We gave alternate versions of the inventory four weeks apart without an introduction to the Enneagram and without introducing any other bias. The analysis revealed a significant concordance, Kappa=0.589 (P <0.0001).